BREAD AND BULLETS
The Rosario Liotta Story

Hook 2019

Rosario Liotta & Donna Carbone

BREAD AND BULLETS

THE ROSARIO LIOTTA STORY

ROSARIO LIOTTA
DONNA M. CARBONE

ROSARIO THE BAKER, INC.

Bread and Bullets is the work of the authors, who have recreated events, locales and conversations from memory. To maintain anonymity in some instances, names of individuals and places have been changed as well as some identifying characteristics and details such as physical properties, occupations and places of residence.

Although the authors have made every effort to ensure that the information in this book was correct at press time, the authors do not assume and hereby disclaim any liability to any party for any loss, damage, or disruption caused by errors or omissions, whether such errors or omissions result from negligence, accident, or any other cause.

Copyright @ 2018 by Rosario The Baker, Inc. All rights reserved. No part of this story may be reproduced or retransmitted in any form or by any electronic or mechanical means, including information storage and retrieval systems, without permission in writing from the author, except by a reviewer who may quote brief passages in a review.

For information contact:
BreadandBullets1949@gmail.com

❀ Created with Vellum

ACKNOWLEDGMENTS

People come and go from your life. Many will call themselves friends, but they only hang around when times are good. There are a few people who have stood beside me and supported me during the hard times. I am eternally grateful.

I want to thank my family for sticking with me during the hardest days of my life: my parents Joan and Vincent Liotta, my wife Sheryl, my children Jimmy and his wife Fiona, Erica and her husband Ozzie, and Rosario Jr., my brother Anthony and my sister Emily and her husband Tony and, of course, all my grandchildren and my mother and father-in-law Carol and Anthony Pappalardo.

I also want to thank my friends: Herschel Adelard, Nick Bimonte, Samantha Cherry, Mike Cody, Richie Hall, Rick Harb, Chuck Lawson, Bob Manino, Mike McClurkin, Al Petrasy, Vito and Victoria Raneri, Donna Scuderi, Lynn and Mike Sharkey, Mike Steinberg, Kenny Tripoli, Jamie Wilson, and the Gio family. Special thanks to kryptonite and all the people who I have unintentionally forgotten to mention. You are all equally important to me.

My attorneys deserve special recognition: David Bogenshultz, Douglas Duncan and Andrew Schwartz. They are all brilliant, ethical men.

Sincere thanks to artist James Hook for creating the cover of *Bread and Bullets* based on the facts of the criminal case. His time and talents are deeply appreciated.B

A special "Thank You" to Donna Carbone, a writer extraordinaire. Convincing her to write my story was no easy task. She turned me down three times but, eventually, my persistence and my belief that she was the right co-author for this book paid off. Donna listened to my stories; she read hundreds of newspaper articles and transcript pages from my trial; she talked to my family and friends. With her gift for words, she was able to not only bring my story to life, she was able to paint a picture of the private me... the one I rarely show to strangers. Donna saw my heart.

I am grateful that, despite having made many mistakes in my life, she recognized that I was more than what was portrayed in the newspapers. I will always be grateful for her friendship and dedication to this project.

PROLOGUE

Funny story.
    I'm very friendly. People like me. I know people you wouldn't expect me to know. My friend, Michael Cody, he never believes me when I say, "I talked to so and so today."

Well, we go to dinner one night at Chamberlain's, the restaurant owned by the great Wilt the Stilt on Glades Road in Boca Raton. It's been closed for years but, back in the day, it was the *in* place to be. Anyway, we go to dinner and on the way, I tell Mike that I know Wilt. He punches me in the arm. "No, you don't." I tell him I do. He bets me $100.00 that I'm lying.

We're having dinner. Guess who walks by. I call out, "Hey, Wilt." He turns, sees me, smiles that big smile of his, and strides across the room, hand extended. "Rosario! How ya been, man?"

Mike slides a $100 bill across the table to me.

A few months later, I'm helping Mike construct a sound system for a political event in Miami. I tell him I know Governor Lawton Chiles, the man who'll be the keynote speaker at this shindig.

Again, he punches me in the arm. "Don't bull shit me, man. You don't know the Governor." I just look at him. He can't resist. "I'll bet you $500 you don't know Governor Chiles." I smile.

Later that night, we're standing in the hotel lobby as the Governor and his entourage come walking through. I make sure I'm in a spot where I'm easily seen. As if on cue, Governor Chiles stops, turns and walks in my direction. "Rosario, what are you doing here?" I'm $500.00 richer.

Now, Mike and me… we decide to take a vacation to Italy. Mike wants to go to the Vatican. I say, "Good idea. I know the Pope." This time he knows I'm lying or, at least, he's pretty sure I'm pulling his leg.

∽

Here's how Mike tells the story.

"We're waiting in the courtyard for the Pope to appear on the balcony. Suddenly, Rosario's gone. I'm looking for him when a roar goes up from the crowd. Everyone is staring up at the balcony cheering. I look up, and who do I see standing next to the Pope? Rosario. I faint.

I don't know how long I was out, but when I open my eyes, Rosario is there looking extremely worried. He says, 'This is all my fault,' and I say, 'Rosario, I never cared about the $100 at Chamberlain's or the $500 in Miami. It wasn't even that you were up there with the Pope. What finally got to me was that everyone down here was asking, 'Who's that guy on the balcony with Rosario?

∽

Despite my address book being filled with page after page of recognizable names and my desire to just live and let live, in 2003 I found myself on the receiving end of a gun. The guy threatening me from the doorway of my store – Rosario's Corner Deli - was a killer. I had no desire to be killed. In self-defense, I grabbed my own gun and fired four times.

My assailant died at the scene. I was arrested for second degree murder but was, eventually, convicted of manslaughter. Ridiculous?

Yes. This was not a case of the facts not speaking clearly in my defense. Plus, I had a witness. Made no difference.

The prosecution argued that I owed my assailant a lot of money - payments on loans he had given me to start my delicatessen. There was some truth to that, but what the jury didn't understand was that his visit that day had nothing to do with me welshing on a debt. He was trying to muscle his way in and take control of not just my business, but my home and family as well. The methods he used... the threats he made... I never doubted for a moment that the home I would be going to at the end of the day would be the county morgue.

This face-to-face standoff with death, which changed my life in so many ways, happened two years before the Stand Your Ground laws went into effect in Florida. Today, I would have walked away a free man.

At trial, I was sentenced to 15 years imprisonment. I served 12. During the 4,380 days I was behind bars, I learned a lot.

Now, I'd like to share my story with you.

CHAPTER ONE

The headline in the New York Times on Thursday, February 8, 2001, read:

South Florida Businessman Killed in Ambush on Street

I barely paid any attention to it. The murder of Miami Subs founder Gus Boulis meant nothing to me. I was too busy running my own business to care why a multi-millionaire entrepreneur with his fingers in a lot of pies had met his death at the bullet end of a gun.

Two years later, on October 30, 2003, the headline in the New York Post, announced:

Gotti Wiseguy is Slain

and under it was my name.

A reputed John Gotti associate, who was acquitted in a 1984 Queens murder, was shot dead at the opening of a Florida delicatessen after threatening to kill the owner, The Post has learned.

Police said (Rosario) Liotta "feared for his life," pulled out a gun and shot three times, sending the one-time Queens tough guy through a glass window in the doorway beneath a large yellow sign that proclaimed, "Grand Opening."

Never for a minute did I imagine a connection between me shooting a hitman for the Gambino crime family and what would eventually become one of the most long-lasting criminal cases in Florida history… a case which took 14 years to come to trial and which brought to light the identity of the alleged gunman – none other than the man I had shot and killed 11 years earlier.

I wasn't arrested at the time of the shooting. I should never have been arrested. The newspapers all reported that the shooting was a clear case of self-defense. Then, the cops came knocking on my door.

Prior to being arrested, my life was in a state of limbo. I felt like a hamster on a wheel, going around and around but getting nowhere. I never wanted to go back to the store; my dreams for the Corner Deli had all been shattered. Plus, there was crime scene tape on everything.

The place held some good memories for me. My son's first birthday party had been held there just three months earlier. The Grand Opening banner was still hanging over the front door. Since the day we officially opened to the public, so many people had stopped in to buy lunch or bring our food home to their families. Old friends and new… I felt like the Corner Deli had found the perfect home.

But, after the shooting, I was uncomfortable. I imagined the other tenants at the Del Mar Shopping Village looking at me and thinking "killer." It was surreal.

That being said, compared to the fear I had felt while my family and I were being threatened, I was at peace. For six months, I was confident that the case would never go to trial. Even after we went to trial, I was confident that I would be acquitted. Boy, was I wrong.

CHAPTER TWO

In 2001, Konstantinos "Gus" Boulis, the founder of Miami Subs and the Sun Cruz Casino line was murdered in cold blood in front of his Fort Lauderdale office. When Boulis exited the building where his office was located, he found his car boxed in. The driver of the car in front of him refused to move; behind him was a car driven by an innocent bystander. A third car approached from the opposite direction. The driver reached out his side window and fired a gun, striking Boulis four times. The road in front of him now clear, Boulis managed to drive onto Federal Highway, where he crashed and died.

The case remained in limbo for a long time; the identity of the killer and those who had hired him unknown. In 2005, after a long and drawn out investigation, Anthony "Big Tony" Moscatiello - a reputed captain of the Gambino crime family and a close friend of the late John Gotti – James "Pudgy" Fiorillo, and Anthony "Little Tony" Ferrari were charged with arranging the hit.

Prosecuting the defendants in this case was complicated as it involved not only members of organized crime, but two high profile businessmen – Washington, D.C. lobbyist Jack Abramoff and New

York businessman Adam Kidan, who was once associated with the popular Dial-a-Mattress company.

If you are the type of person who wants to know all the facts, then the mention of Abramoff's name should have your nose twitching. Jack Abramoff's scandal-filled life has been the subject of two films – Casino Jack, a Hollywood feature film starring Kevin Spacey, and the documentary Casino Jack and the United States of Money, written by Alex Gibney.

On the internet, he is listed as a businessman and lobbyist. The truth is he was a con man who swindled his way to fame, fortune and a prison sentence. To quote Neil Volz, a former associate, "Jack Abramoff could sweet-talk a dog off a meat truck."

Kidan, who was a close friend of Abramoff, became his business partner in the SunCruz Casino deal. Gus Boulis died because these two men and their associates had no scruples. Greed was their only God.

The story of Gus Boulis' demise began in 1990. He founded SunCruz Casinos – a fleet of 11 ships which offered "cruises to nowhere" and allowed passengers to gamble outside Florida's three-mile limit. The company brought in millions of dollars a year, but unbeknownst to Boulis, his participation in the venture was illegal under a little-known law which barred foreigners from owning American commercial vessels. He had no choice but to sell.

An offer came from Abramoff and Kidan, who falsely represented to bank officials, investors and the federal government their intention to buy SunCruz Casinos from Boulis for the sum of $147.5 million. Boulis agreed to the deal but never saw any payments. He grew frustrated and, eventually, realized that he was being scammed. Threats were exchanged and Kidan filed for a restraining order in late 2000.

Under interrogation, Kidan told investigators that Boulis had threatened to kill him and, in fear for his life, he had reached out to the mob for help. His "protectors" were Anthony Moscatiello and Anthony Ferrari, a low-level mobster who claimed to be the nephew of John Gotti.

The deal between Kidan and these men was simple. He would purchase wine to be sold on the SunCruz ships from Moscatiello's legally owned distributorship as well as hire Ferrari's security company, Moon Over Miami Beach. The money was really meant to keep Kidan alive as no one (in this case Boulis) could hire the mob to kill someone the mob was already protecting.

At the end of his rope, Boulis petitioned the court to regain control of SunCruz. The bull's eye was now on Boulis' back because if his petition was recognized by the court, Moscatiello stood to lose a lot of money. Enter Peter "Bud" Zaccaro, a confessed hit man who turned state's evidence and testified that Big Tony had hired him to kill Boulis.

According to Zaccaro, he refused the job because the motive was money. In his testimony, he stated, "If it was principle, you killed them. If you killed people for money, it was cursed. I didn't kill people for money. Principle, yes. Money, no."

Zaccaro was put into the witness protection program. The gunman who took the job of killing Gus Boulis… his childhood friend, John Gurino.

This is where the Boulis case and my life intersect.

CHAPTER THREE

There was a time when I was a simple baker. Well, maybe, not so simple. I grew a one-van business into a million-dollar venture. Rosario's Flatbread Crackers, Inc. started out as a small operation. I supplied crackers to restaurants and hotels in Dade, Broward and Palm Beach Counties. As my reputation grew, so did demand for my products.

When I started my bread business years later, two trucks quickly became 16 trucks and my territory ranged from the Florida Keys to the Georgia line in Jacksonville. On the east coast of the Sunshine State, I was rolling in dough… literally.

If you've eaten at J. Alexanders, Ruth's Chris Steakhouse, Duffy's, the Ale Houses, Flanigan's, California Pizza Kitchen, any of the big hotels and country clubs, you've eaten my bread. For 10 years, I had the Midas touch. Every venture I undertook became a success. That was before I shot John Gurino. After that, crumbs were all that were left of the life I knew.

When I got out of prison in 2014, the world I had left no longer existed. It took a lot of adjusting. My wife, Sheryl, thankfully, stayed at my side, and my kids… well, they are my pride and joy. Smart kids. Maybe smarter than me.

Twelve years in the joint, I learned a lot. Before going in, I was street wise. Coming out, I had a doctorate in the laws of the jungle.

Forget everything you've ever seen in a Hollywood movie. Real prison is a thousand times worse than that. Everybody hates everybody. Racism and corruption are rampant.

Going to prison was an education on so many levels. I had to learn how to be a chameleon… when to be tough and when to be quiet. In prison, you are constantly in survival mode.

I've always been a hard worker. I used that work ethic while I was on the inside, and it served me well. People – inmates and guards – respected me because I always kept my word.

Now that I'm free, I'm an even harder worker. Emotionally, I'm stronger. Physically, too, but there are nights I'm so tired when I get home from my job, my family must help me out of my car. My feet and my body ache so badly I can't move. I'm not complaining.

I made mistakes. I know I hurt a lot of people – especially my wives. Yes, more than one. My actions were never intentional.

If you were a teenager during the 1950s, you probably remember the song *Devil or Angel*. Some of the lyrics were "Devil or angel, I can't make up my mind which one you are." I think that's how my wives felt about me. I was a bit of both, and it wasn't necessarily an even distribution of character traits.

While I loved each of them and wanted – still want - only the best for them, sometimes that horned guy in the red suit made me do some unforgivable things.

For that, I'm sorry.

The neighborhood on Long Island where I grew up was in the heart of North Babylon's *Little Italy*. Just blocks from my front door was Zito's market, where Italian immigrants gathered every day to exchange stories about the old country and catch up on local gossip. This was long before the term "latch key kids" became popular or anyone thought of the idea that it takes a village. Every adult was an honorary aunt or uncle and God help us kids if we weren't respectful.

I wasn't a good student. Being dyslexic, I was left back a few times. The first time was in the first grade. If you don't suffer from this condition, you have no idea what it's like to be a kid struggling to read and write. My real friends... the kids from my neighborhood... were kind to me, but some of the other kids were just plain mean. I failed every test, and with every failure, the teasing got worse.

My parents spent half their time in the principal's office, but even he had no idea what was wrong. In those days, no one knew about dyslexia and how it affected kids. Eventually, the school arranged for a psychologist to give me a battery of tests.

I'll never forget that day. Just knowing that someone was going to analyze me made me feel like I was damaged in some way. I remember thinking I must be so stupid to have been left back in first grade.

On the day of the testing, two psychologists – a man and a woman – described for my mom and dad what they were about to do. While they were talking, I sat at a table where random puzzle pieces were spread about. There were a lot of them from four or five different jigsaw puzzles all mixed together. I amused myself by putting the puzzles together. The male psychologist was watching me, but I didn't know that.

Eventually, my mom and dad left and the two therapists began their analysis. They had me take a Rorschach test. I didn't understand why they cared what I saw in the blobs of ink. It seemed weird. When they were finished, they told my parents I was brilliant. They were most impressed by how I had put all the puzzles together.

Being brilliant didn't change anything. I still couldn't read or write without struggling, and continually getting left back was painful. All my neighborhood friends moved up while I stayed behind. Since school was only a few blocks from my house, every day I had to hear my pals talk about things I would never get to do. It hurt and made me feel even more stupid.

When just going to school is traumatic, you start to build a shield around yourself. I didn't realize it then, but my disposition was changing. I was still funny – I used to hide behind a sense of humor... the class clown – but now I also hid the anger I felt when people were cruel to me. In time, the anger had to come out and I began to fight back. Sometimes, with my fists.

It got worse as I got older. In junior high, I took a bus to school. The kids would torment me by holding a book up close to my face and asking if I could read it. They would say, "Liotta, show us you can read. Come on, tell us what this word is." Remember, I might have only been in junior high, but I was years older than my classmates. I was a lot bigger and stronger. The school bus driver spent a portion of every trip to and from school pulling me off another kid.

When I was 16, I dropped out. I was already working at my dad's bakery and making good money. I owned a car and was able to come and go as I pleased. The days of being a schoolboy were over.

During the day, I worked hard. At night, I hung out with my friends. Think *The Lords of Flatbush*. If you've never seen that movie, you should watch it. I was a lot like the Butchey Weinstein character, played by Henry Winkler. Despite never getting a higher education, I was always smart when it came to business, but I hid my brains behind a sense of humor that had everyone thinking I was a clown. That was the best lesson I learned in school.

Now that I'm an adult and have adapted to my dyslexia, I can look back and see what the school was doing wrong. If I was interested in a subject and the teacher wrote on the blackboard, I learned quickly, but if we were reading from a text book, my attention wandered. Struggling to put letters together to make words was difficult. By the time I figured out a complete sentence, the class was two chapters ahead. Taking notes in class was useless because I couldn't make sense of them when I got home.

I couldn't spell... still can't spell... because coming from New York, I pronounce words differently. Window is winda. Soda is soder. Syrup is searup. Coffee is cawfee. Huge is yuuge. Newark is Nwork. It's a good thing someone else is writing this book or you would be struggling to learn a foreign language.

I taught myself to read by using the Reader's Digest and gossip newspapers. The stories were short and interesting. I didn't get bored. In time, I became a sight reader, memorizing the words. Cell phones are the greatest invention. At work, if someone calls in an order, I can repeat it into the records on the phone and replay it for the sales help. No mistakes.

Show me a diagram and I'm an expert at whatever is being built. Let me watch someone do anything – build, draw, paint – and I can recreate it. Take me on a road trip and I will remember the route. When I see or hear something that interests me, I commit it to memory.

There are a lot of things I wish I could forget, but the curse of over-compensating for dyslexia means I have almost instant recall.

When I was in prison, I read *In the Mind's Eye* by Thomas West. It was amazing and helped me to understand how different style and size fonts, different color paper and print, lights and shadows… so many things… make it difficult for people with dyslexia to read. Albert Einstein, Thomas Edison, Lewis Carroll and Winston Churchill were all sight readers. Like me, they processed information in terms of images instead of words and numbers. I'm not saying I'm as smart as they were, but those psychologists back in first grade did say I was "brilliant."

CHAPTER FOUR

*E*very high school – past, present and future – is in competition with the neighboring high schools. Mostly, it's sports related... whose football or basketball team is the best. Sometimes girls take center court. The rivalries make for some interesting pranks being pulled on the unsuspecting.

Whenever it rained, my best friend Nicky, me and our pals would drive over to the bus stop where the kids from our biggest rival waited to be picked up. Mostly, Nicky drove because his car was big enough for all of us to fit inside with room to spare. Because drainage was so bad in certain parts of the city, there was always a huge puddle at the corner closest to the bus stop. There were lots of kids from every grade waiting to go to school. They were the perfect targets.

Nicky would come around the corner at full speed and drive through that puddle so fast the water shot out like a fire hose. Anyone standing within 10 feet got soaked. No matter how often we did it, those kids never learned. After every storm the puddle was there and every morning the crowd stood on that corner just asking for a bath. What is that quote about insanity... that it's doing the same thing over and over again expecting different results? There must have been a lot of nutty kids in that neighborhood.

One morning, after a really bad storm, we pulled the same stunt. The water was so deep, it splashed back onto the car windshield making it impossible to see. My buddies and I screamed at Nicky to turn on his wipers. Only problem... when he had his car detailed the day before, the car wash guys forgot to put the wiper blades back on. All we heard was the scratch and screech as the metal arms went back and forth across the glass.

We couldn't see a thing. Nicky hit the brakes, but it was too late. He smashed head on into another car. The kids at the bus stop saw their chance, and they started running towards the crash. We knew we were going to get our asses kicked so we took off.

When we came back to get the car a few hours later, it was destroyed. The bumpers were kicked in. The tires were slashed. Every window was broken. It looked like a stolen vehicle that had been stripped for parts. Nicky was upset but truth be told, we deserved it.

You would think we'd have learned from that incident, but the next storm, we did it again. This time we used my car. I made sure the wiper blades worked before we pulled out of the driveway. I guess insanity wasn't confined to just one neighborhood.

When I was 17, I met Tina and thought I was in love. We dated for a long time but, eventually, the relationship ended. Since I hung out with the high school crowd, I got invited to all the dances and parties. That's how I met Barbara. I was immediately attracted to her, but she was dating some other guy, so we only said "Hi" when we saw each other.

Barbara had three sisters; their mom had brought them to New York from Kentucky. I never knew the full reason why their dad wasn't in the picture, but I always suspected he wasn't a good guy. Barbara had blonde hair and soft brown eyes. She was a genuinely nice person. When she spoke, it was with a soft country/southern twang. Compared to my New York accent, it was sweet on the ears.

When Barbara and her boyfriend broke up, we started dating. I fell in love for real this time. We wanted to move in together, but Barbara's mother read us the holy hell act from the bible. The only way we were going to sleep in the same bed every night was to get married, so that's what we did. We were 19 at the time.

With the benefit of hindsight, I'd have to say that I got married because everyone was doing it. Teenagers were a lot different in the 1970s than they are now. For one thing, we talked a lot about having sex, but we rarely actually did it. Sex wasn't treated with the carefree attitude that we have today. People went to church where a heavy dose of guilt was served along with the Communion wafer.

I loved Barbara, but I was too immature to understand the responsibilities that came with being a husband. I was cocky. Truthfully, I was an asshole; I didn't take my marriage vows seriously. Thought they were meant for her, but I could do whatever I wanted.

Working the long hours that I put in for dad's bakery business, I was always uptight at the end of the day, and the end of the day for me was the early hours of the morning. I went to work when most people were going to bed, and I went to sleep when other people were going about their daily routines. Barbara and I were on totally different schedules.

By the weekend, the only thing I wanted was to have a good time. Staying home and doing family stuff, which is what Barbara preferred, just didn't appeal to me.

We were only married a few months when I started to step out on her. It wasn't really a question of cheating; more a matter of indiscretions. I loved to dance; this was the disco era, but Barbara never wanted to go to the clubs with me. I went with my guy friends, and I would flirt with the girls we met. I hate myself for doing it, but I can't hide from the truth.

I remember this one time near the end of our marriage... Barbara and I had been together about six years. It was winter – close to the Christmas holidays – and there was a layer of snow on the ground. I was driving the Lotus, which you will hear more about later in this story. The roads were bad but my buddies and me, we decided to go to a club.

Because of the weather, the place was practically empty when we got there. Since the club was one of our favorite hangouts, we were friendly with the owner/bartender. His name was John. We ordered a few rounds and had a few laughs. I felt good… relaxed.

To our left was a guy with two good-looking girls. I told John to buy the girls a drink… not the guy, just the girls. He shook his head at me; asked me not to make any trouble. The guy and one of the girls were an item.

In time, we got tired of sitting at the bar, so we took our drinks and moved over to a more secluded area where there were couches and comfortable chairs. After a few minutes, one of the girls – the girl who wasn't with the guy - walked over and sat down next to me. We started to flirt with each other. The conversation went something like this:

"I hear you wanted to buy me a drink, but you never said 'Hello.'"

"I was busy, but I knew you would come over sooner or later."

"You're pretty sure of yourself."

"You're here, aren't you?"

"You're an asshole."

I agreed.

She stayed with me, and we had a few more drinks. Meanwhile, the other girl wanted to leave but didn't want her friend to make the trip home to Lindenhurst by herself. Lindenhurst was on the south shore of Long Island and, in winter, the trip could be hazardous. I promised I would see her home safely.

This girl… she was so beautiful, and I told her so. I couldn't keep my eyes and, eventually, my hands off her. Wanting to impress her, I said, "Let's do something crazy. How about a trip to Atlantic City?"

Her eyes got so big; she asked my buddies if I was serious and they assured her I was. Three hours later, we arrived in the gambling capital of New Jersey.

Before we returned to Long Island, I called my dad and he warned me that I was in trouble. The warning was unnecessary since this was not unusual behavior for me. When I dropped the girl back at her house, I noticed that my shirt was covered in lipstick. I took it off and threw it out the car window, quickly turning the heater on full blast.

Back home, I took a clean shirt out of the dryer while Barbara watched from the kitchen. She asked me, "Where the hell have you been?" That's when I noticed a gun on the table beside her. My normal cockiness evaporated quickly.

After exchanging a barrage of four letter words, we both agreed we couldn't go on the way we were living. I wasn't going to change, and we both knew it. She deserved a man who would be faithful and love her for the rest of her life. That just wasn't me. A divorce was the only solution. I went upstairs to our bedroom to pack.

At the time I moved out of the house, I owned a Harley low rider, the Lotus, a Monte Carlo and the bread truck. I planned to keep the Lotus and the truck, which I needed for work. Barbara would keep the Monte Carlo. Unfortunately, the insurance for the Lotus was in Barbara's name, which technically made her the owner.

While I was packing, my wife called her mother, who called the police. The police tried to stop me from taking the car, but by then, I had smashed the air valves with a sledge hammer. Don't know how I didn't get arrested. I got in the truck and took off.

A few hours later, Barbara came to my parent's house and said she didn't want to breakup. I told her again that I wasn't going to change.

In the meantime, my dad called from the bakery and told me to take possession of the Lotus. When I got there, the cops were waiting along with Barbara and her mother. After a few heated words, she agreed that I could buy the car from her. I had to take out a loan to pay her off, but the Lotus was finally mine.

Barbara did not deserve the way I treated her. As contentious as those last days together were for us, we're now good friends. When last we saw each other, more than 20 years after our divorce, she said she still cared about me. Her exact words were, "I love you, Rosario. You're a great guy. You're just a lousy husband."

She got no argument from me.

CHAPTER FIVE

*B*y winter 1979, Barbara and I were going through a messy divorce. Kimberly was my new girlfriend. Kimberly worked at Feed and Grain, a popular club in Northport on Long Island. Northport is a historic maritime village surrounded by hills. The main street, where the clubs are located, runs along the harbor. It's beautiful. I spent a lot of nights there so I could be close to Kim.

Everybody at Feed and Grain knew me and they knew my car. One Sunday night while partying with my buddy Nick, I decided to take the ride to Northport because I missed Kimberly. It just so happened that the Lotus was in the shop for service. When I brought it in to the dealership, the manager gave me a four-door Peugeot sedan as a loaner. That's what I was driving when this incident happened.

Nick didn't want to go with me to Northport, but another guy who was with us asked if he could tag along. He had never been to that area and had heard great thing about it. Northport is a 45 minute drive from North Babylon, and I didn't want to be responsible for bringing this guy home at the end of the night. I told him to follow me to my house, where he could leave his car in the driveway. I knew somebody at the club would give him a ride back.

Feed and Grain had different levels for dining and dancing. Each level required climbing an outside staircase to gain access. When we arrived, I parked the car out front and immediately saw Kim on the upper deck with two guys. It was obvious that one of the guys was putting the moves on her, while the other guy egged him on. Kim kept trying to get away but the guy was aggressive. I was getting more pissed by the minute. I took my gun out of my boot and handed it to my passenger. I told him to hold onto it and stay in the car.

Because I wasn't driving the Lotus, Kimberly didn't realize I was there. I got out of the car and started up the stairs. As I was nearing the top, I saw the guy grab Kim's face and try to kiss her. She was fighting him. My head exploded. I grabbed a 2x4 that was lying nearby and ran the rest of the way up the stairs. They whack I gave him sent him flying. He was out cold. His friend ran into the club with me close behind. The bouncers had seen what happened outside and tried to stop me, but I was too fast for them. I grabbed the scumbag and smashed his head into the juke box.

The bouncers surrounded me and pulled me off him. They knew I had a gun permit and thought I was carrying. I was uncontrollable, so the management called for bouncers from other bars in the area to help. I knew I had to get out of there.

In my hurry to escape, I jumped down a flight of stairs, breaking my ankle. The pain was excruciating. As I limped to the car, people scattered. The guy who rode up with me was white as a ghost. He tried to get out of the car, but I held him back. He kept begging me to let him go.

To leave Northport, I had to drive down the street directly in front of the bar. Before I was out of the parking lot, I could see police cars heading my way. They had set up a roadblock at each corner. The guy in the car shoved my gun into my hand; I put it under the seat. I told him that whatever happened, he should pretend to be mute. Since he was scared shitless, keeping him quiet wasn't going to be a problem.

Deciding to act as if I knew nothing, I drove up to the roadblock and asked one of the cops what was happening. The cop was non-committal. He merely said they were looking for a little black sports car and asked if we had seen anything fitting that description. Of course, I said we hadn't so he let us through. FYI: he was asking about the Lotus so in a sense, I wasn't lying.

Once we got to the Southern State Parkway, the guy started begging me again to let him out of the car. I stopped and he jumped out. I never saw him again.

Okay. So, my right ankle was broken. The pain was getting worse by the minute. My foot was swollen into my boot, and the boot was the only thing keeping the bones together. I could barely drive, but I managed to get myself to Good Samaritan Hospital, which was in West Islip near my house. I called my dad and told him I was in trouble. No details needed. My dad knew I had fucked up.

The cops knew my identity because everyone at the bar knew me. In the morning, they went to the bakery, but I didn't go to work. My dad didn't know where I was so he couldn't tell them anything. I knew it was best to keep him in the dark. The cops gave dad a subpoena for me to appear in court. He hired Anthony Gazzara, the brother of actor Ben Gazzara, to be my lawyer. Court was in Northport. Through some connections, we learned that the father of the asshole I hit was the mayor of Huntington, the town next to Northport. Word was that both town's officials wanted me bad!

Dad got some of his friends to accompany us on the day of the hearing. In the courtroom, people were staring at me like I was Charles Manson. When my case was called, the judge read me the riot act. He said, "You can't come into our city, beat up our citizens and think you're going to get away with it.

He then asked the prosecutor to show him the arrest report and my rap sheet. The prosecutor handed him the rap sheet but had to admit that I had never been arrested. The judge was furious. Two months had passed since the incident at Feed and Grain, and I had never been arrested. He started screaming, "You take him in the back and book him now." My attorney objected and asked to approach the bench.

Anthony argued that since I had never been arrested, there was no proof I was the guilty party. He was right. The judge slammed his gavel down and ordered the lawyers into his office. An hour passed during which we could hear them arguing. When the returned, the judge's face was scarlet. He dismissed the case with the warning, "If you come up the Jericho Turnpike, don't come into Huntington because I will find a reason to arrest you."

When we left the courthouse, we were hungry. Victory can do that to you. My dad refused to eat anywhere in Northport. He wanted to head back home. That's when the day got even more interesting.

Dad had just bought a brand new Bill Blass Lincoln Continental Mark IV. The car was a beauty. We pulled out of the courthouse parking lot with dad's friends following close behind. Remember I told you that Northport was a harbor town surrounded by hills? Well, there were a lot of boats being transported on trailers up and down those hills.

As my dad was going up one particularly steep hill, there was a boat ahead of him slowing traffic. I kept nudging him to pass the boat on the right. He didn't want to do it, but I kept insisting. Against his better judgment, he moved over, passed the boat, and when we came to the top of the hill, he stopped for a red light. Problem was that the boat was so big, he couldn't see anything coming from the left.

The light turned green and my dad hit the gas. A car coming from the other side ran the red light and slammed into the Lincoln, totaling it. Dad kicked me out of the car and told me to ride home with his friends. He stayed and waited for the cops alone because he knew this was just the excuse they needed to get me back in court.

CHAPTER SIX

"Rules are for the obedience of fools and interpretations of smart men."
~Colin Chapman~
(designer/builder of Lotus Mark 1 – 1948)

*H*ere's another Lotus story.

My sister was having a party in Lindenhurst; I don't remember the occasion. She invited my wife Barbara even though we were separated. Barbara was wearing an absolutely beautiful dress... sexy... and she made it clear she wanted me back. I kept telling her I wasn't interested as I was already involved with a new girlfriend, Kimberly. I told Barbara to put me out of her mind. I was only there so my sister wouldn't be mad. After a drink or two, I was planning to leave.

Kimberly lived about 45 minutes north of Lindenhurst. Between the coke and the drinks, I was driving the Sunken Meadow Parkway like it was the Indy 500. The Lotus had a small rear window. In the dark, it was especially hard to see anything in the rearview mirror. The radio was playing and I was singing along, oblivious to the flashing lights in the distance that were gradually getting closer. I stopped at a red light and, suddenly, was surrounded by police cars. I was wearing jeans and had two grams of cocaine in the coin pocket. As was my custom, my .38 was in my boot.

Needless to say, my first thought as I patted the vial of coke was "Oh, shit!"

The cops pulled me out of the car and handcuffed me. They took my wallet out of my back pants pocket and started looking through it. I had a habit of asking every cop, judge and lawyer I ever met for their business card. Didn't matter how I had met them. Those cards were in my wallet.

Whenever I needed help, I would pull out a card and act like the person named on it was my best friend. On this night, a lieutenant took special notice of one of the cards. He held it up to my face and asked why I had it. I didn't really know what he meant. Why does anyone have someone else's business card? It just so happened that the card he was holding belonged to the chief of police.

Feeling cornered, I got a little mouthy and said, "You want to give me a ticket, give me a ticket. You want to arrest me, arrest me. I wasn't trying to get away from you. Would I have stopped at a fucking red light if I was trying to escape?"

The lieutenant kept waving the card in my face and asking why I had it. I said, "Look. Just arrest me. Then, you'll see why I have that card." I was ballsy.

With a sneer on his face, he turned away to talk to the other cops and when he came back, he said, "This is what we're going to do. We're going to move your car into that parking lot (a strip mall was nearby) and I'll leave an officer here to protect it. You're coming to the precinct with me."

Off we went. They didn't search me. I still had the gun and the coke. At the precinct, they uncuffed me and sat me on a bench with a bunch of other guys who have been arrested. I managed to get the vial out of my pocket without being obvious. There was a guy sitting a few feet away who looked like he could use a fix. "Hey, buddy," I said just loud enough for him to hear. "Catch this." The vial passed between us and no one was the wiser. He thanked me like I had done him a big favor.

Eventually, the lieutenant came back and said I could leave but since they hadn't been able to reach anyone who could confirm my identity, they were keeping my license and registration. How I was supposed to get home? After a little back and forth on the issue, I told them I was meeting my girlfriend at Images, a local club. The lieutenant insisted that an officer would drive me there. That club was aptly named that night. Just imagine what the long line of waiting patrons thought when I arrived in a police car.

I found Kimberly and told her what had happened. She asked a friend to drive us back to my car. When we got there, the cop on duty gave me back my keys and left. He had made it clear that he expected Kim to drive my car home. Of course, that didn't happen. Kim and her friend went back to Images. I waved goodbye as I pulled out of the parking lot.

Three days later I got a call from the precinct. It was the chief of police whose card I had in my wallet. He said, "Mr. Liotta, please come into the precinct and pick up your wallet and registration and don't ever come into my town again."

CHAPTER SEVEN

"When I die, I want to come back as me. I've had a good life."

My earliest memories are of flour and yeast. My father, Vincenzo Liotta, was a baker. At least, that was his legit job. He was also a bookie. He had 10 or 12 guys under him who collected the bets.

In the beginning, my dad worked for Martin Bakery. The owner of the bakery had two brothers. One of them worked for my dad running numbers. Next to the bakery was a big butcher shop. The owner's name was Albee or something like that. A lot of Italians from the neighborhood shopped there.

Albee also worked for my dad, taking numbers at his store. He was making a lot of money, but instead of keeping a low profile as was the custom, he bought a beautiful brand new red El Dorado convertible with white interior and kept it parked in front of the store. The car got a lot of attention.

~

For those of you who did not grow up in cities where organized crime held sway, playing the numbers was a form of illegal gambling wherein a bettor attempts to pick three digits to match those that will be randomly drawn the following day. Seven days a week, a gambler could place a bet at a bar, tavern, barber shop, social club or any other semi-private place that acted as an illegal betting parlor. A runner then carried the money and betting slips between the betting parlors and the numbers bank (headquarters), where it was logged and tracked.

People in lower income Italian and black neighborhoods played the numbers in the hope of a better future. They were dreamers just like the people who play the lottery today.

Growing up, there wasn't a kid over six who didn't know what it meant when their mom handed them a slip of paper and said, "Take this to So-and-So and tell him I want to play it straight (or box it)."

If numbers are boxed, it doesn't matter in which order you pick them just as long as you pick all three.

In inner city neighborhoods, so-and-so was probably the guy who owned the corner grocery store or drove the fresh vegetable truck that made its way through the streets every day. He could live next door to you or be a stranger. His name wasn't important. All that mattered was the little black book he kept in his pocket to write down your wager.

Some people played as little as a penny. Others might play a $1.00. A lot of those dollars were bet on credit, and just like today, the vig (interest) could be hefty. I can't remember knowing anyone who won.

Early on, I had no idea that my father ran numbers. Most kids had no idea their parents were gambling; don't think most of them would have cared if they had known. It was just a part of growing up in the inner city.

Hollywood has made lots of mob movies and in almost every one of them, the Don warns his soldiers and captains not to flash their money around. There's a reason for that. The less people know about you, the better. Because of the car, people began to know much too much about Albee. Among the people taking notice were the Feds. He got arrested, but it was kept hush hush. We didn't know anything until government agents came knocking on our door. I vividly remember that day.

The elementary school my brother and I attended was only three blocks from our house. One day when I was in sixth or seventh grade, my mom picked us up in the car and drove us home. I don't remember why; she hardly ever did that.

When we got to our house, we found cops running all over the neighborhood. Albee had saved his own ass by ratting everybody else out, even the guys in the head office. Heads were going to roll.

Mom pulled the car half way into a space and jumped out. Dad could be seen sitting handcuffed in the back of a police car, and Mom started screaming. My father kept putting his hand to his heart as if to say, "Stop. I'm okay." I know she didn't believe him because she was crying hysterically.

One of the cops came over and pulled my mother away from the car. She wanted to go inside the house, but the cop wouldn't let her. She kept trying to get to the backyard where our dog, a French poodle, was yapping at the gate. Again, the cop held her back.

Time passed. I was hungry and had to go to the bathroom, but I was afraid to leave my mother's side. By the time the cops left, the house was unlivable. They had ransacked every square inch. Furniture was turned upside down; the sofa cushions were torn open. Dishes and lamps were broken; even the food from the refrigerator was thrown on the floor.

My dad was what they called the banker. All the money collected was kept in a safe concealed in the floor of the master bedroom closet. The cops found it and tore it out. What a mess!

My parents weren't the only ones caught up in the sting that day. My father's brother and his wife as well as many of our friends were unprepared for the raid.

Back then, all the bets were listed in a notebook. The notebook was how the bookmaker knew who and how much someone owed and what to pay out. When the Feds raided my uncle's house, they found my aunt tearing pages out of a notebook and flushing them down the toilet. She was arrested and sent to until bail was posted. My aunt is deceased now, but she never forgot those three days spent in hell on earth.

When the Long Island NEWSDAY local paper came out in the morning, there were huge headlines announcing how the Feds had successfully arrested members of a crime family, including a local baker, for running numbers. They called it *OPERATION DOUGHBOY*.

At school, all the kids knew what had happened. Some of them had a copy of the newspaper with them. They looked at me like I was a stranger, someone they had never met before. A few "friends" treated me differently, as if I was a bad person because of what my dad had done.

The outcome of Operation Doughboy was that dad was put on probation. He never served as much as a day in prison. The bakery was still doing business, and our lives went on much as they had before the bust.

I've never forgotten what it felt like to be punished unfairly for something that someone else had done. As you will see, that became a recurring theme in my life.

So, as I said, my earliest memories are of flour and yeast and watching my dad take numbers. The numbers meant nothing to me, but the bakery… that's where my life lessons began, especially the one about the value of hard work.

I have so many great stories from those early days. I still get excited when I open a fresh loaf of bread and inhale the doughy aroma. I swear, if a woman was to dab a little yeast behind her ears… well, in my case, the winner of the battle between the sexes has always been pre-determined. At last count, I've been married three times and engaged one other time.

I was 14 in 1971 when my Dad opened the Sunshine Bakery in North Babylon, Long Island. My first job was feeding the dough into the kneading machine. It was boring, but it paid well. I earned $300 a week, a lot of money for a kid my age. Once I turned 16 and got my driver's license, I became the delivery guy and the salesman. Selling was in my DNA.

∼

Quick story about my dad:

He was a quiet man, but he was tough. As a marine, he wasn't afraid of anyone or anything. He especially wasn't going to take any crap from a smart-mouthed teenaged son who thought he knew all there was to know about life. Imagine me… smart mouthed? Hard to believe, right?

I used to pick on my younger brother Anthony mercilessly. Nothing my parents said could stop the abuse. Anthony would cry and I would laugh. That's what older brothers do. Teasing is a sign of affection. At least, that's what I told my father.

On a sunny Saturday morning, Anthony and I got into another punching match. I was older and bigger so he didn't have much of a chance against me. My dad was pissed. He screamed at me from the back door, "Get over here!" One look at his face and I knew I was in deep shit. My dad had a habit of biting his fist when he was furious. He would mutter half out loud, "I'm gonna kill you." This time he wasn't muttering. There was murder in his eyes. I took off running.

A stockade fence separated our backyard from the neighbor's yard. It must have been six or seven feet high. I don't know how I did it, but I scaled that fence like an Olympic high jumper. I thought I had outsmarted my father and that he would never be able to catch me. A quick glance behind me, and I knew that my old man wasn't so old. He cleared that fence like a gazelle. I think that was the only time I was ever really scared in my life.

At top speed, I took off down the road that ran in front of my high school. My father was on my heels. How was it that in 16 years, I had never seen my father run? Ignorance was no longer bliss. When I look back, I can laugh at how comical we must have appeared to my buddies who were playing football on the school field. I thought my dad would stop chasing me because he wouldn't want people to see him hit me. Wrong.

I started yelling over my shoulder, "Dad, stop! My friends are going to see you." He didn't even slow down. Once we were past the field, he closed the gap between us and beat the crap out of me (not really but it sure seemed like it then). I deserved it.

CHAPTER EIGHT

*I*n the world where I grew up, everyone had a nickname. You know some of them... Al "Scarface" Capone, Charles "Lucky" Luciano, Benjamin "Bugsy" Siegel, Joseph "Joe Bananas" Bonanno, Albert "Mad Hatter" Anastasia, Arthur "Dutch Schultz" Flegenheimer, and John "Teflon Don" Gotti.

I had a nickname, too, but I got it for a much different reason. Where those guys were violent, I had a knack for words. My friends... the people who knew me well... called me The Negotiator.

Thanks to Hollywood movies, the public's perception of organized crime is to shoot first and ask questions later. In some cases, that was true, especially in decades past, but there were many instances where words were the currency exchanged. One of the reasons I love *The Godfather* movies so much is because they show Vito Corleone as a man who understood the value of talking through a tough situation. Of course, in order for words to work, you have to know what to say and how to say it. There also has to be *something* behind the words as backup. That's where I excelled.

Rarely did I have to employ *something* other than my voice. When I did, I only needed to do it once. I never backed away from a fight, but I never instigated one either. I broke my hand three times, each time because some jackass didn't know enough to shut his mouth. Stupid people become aggressive when they are cornered instead of just paying what they owe. Most of the people I was sent to talk to were quick learners. Here's an example.

There were two guys named Louie... Louie the Greek and Louie the Italian. The Greek owed the Italian money. Not a lot but enough that the Italian was anxious to be repaid. The Greek owned a few high-end diners on Long Island. He was making a good income and should not have been delinquent with his payments. It's amazing how stupid some smart business people can be.

Louie the Italian and I were friends. Since Louie lived a long distance from the Greek's diners and I lived close by, he asked me to stop in and *request* the money he was owed. I did a little advance background checking and found out that I actually knew Louie the Greek. Although married, he had a girlfriend and he and his goumada (mistress) often hung out at the same clubs where my buddies and I would party. Since Long Island is a small world, it didn't surprise me to learn that the Greek's girlfriend's sister was dating my brother.

One morning, I paid a visit to the diner closest to my hunting grounds. I asked if Louie was there and was told he would be in shortly. I waited and waited and waited. I waited so long I decided to eat lunch. Still, I waited. He never showed up. Didn't take a genius to figure out that the diner manager had given him a heads up.

When it came time to pay the bill, I decided to write a note to Louie on a napkin. "Our mutual friend has been trying to reach you, but you never return his calls. I'll be back tomorrow." I gave the note to the manager and left without paying.

The next day, the same thing happened. This time, I told the counter guy to call Louie so I could talk to him on the phone.

"Listen, Louie. You were supposed to be here. If you weren't coming, you should have left something for me to give to my friend."

Louie sounded agitated. "Okay. Okay. I'll get it."

I said, "Just tell me where and when you want to meet, and I'll be there."

Now, Louie was really nervous. "Don't come to me. I'll take care of it."

"Okay. Call my friend today. He's anxious to hear from you."

Notice the word *money* was never mentioned.

I knew Louie has no intention of settling his debt. Every day I went to the diner, and every day I brought eight or ten friends with me. We'd eat dinner; I'd sign the bill and leave without paying. If someone tried to stop us, I'd say, "Louie knows about it. Call him."

Came the night when the manager did call Louie and we talked on the phone... again. Louie said he would meet me at the diner the next day at noon. Of course, that never happened.

Through my brother's girlfriend, I found out that Louie lived in Dix Hills, a really ritzy section of Long Island. When Louie didn't show up at the diner, I drove to his house and waited outside. I was there about an hour when a car pulled into the driveway. A woman and two kids were inside. When the woman got out of the car, I approached her and very politely asked if Louie was home. She said he would be there shortly. I offered to help her carry the grocery bags which were in the trunk of the car to the front door. She was grateful.

While I was being the Good Samaritan, Louie drove up. He was furious to see me with his family. I thought he was going to have a nervous breakdown. "You come to my house! You come to my house and bother my wife and kids!" His face was tomato red.

I let him rant. When he came up for air, I said, "I'm a nice guy. I helped your wife with the groceries. That's it. Now, what do you want to do?"

He was shaking all over. "Tomorrow, you come to the diner at noon."

I did. He was there and he paid every cent he owed to Louie the Italian.

You know that old adage, *Actions speak louder than words*? Saint Anthony of Padua said that. The rest of the quote is *Let your words teach and your actions speak*. Me and Saint Anthony... we think alike.

Remember I said that Long Island is a small world?

Wee Scotty's was a popular nightclub that played the oldies. I liked to hang out there. On one of those nights, I saw Louie the Greek at the bar with his girlfriend, Cindy. She was beautiful. I decided to join the group of people Louie was telling that he had bought Cindy a new Oldsmobile. He was a braggart and was so into himself that he didn't recognize me.

Cindy and I struck up a conversation, and it was obvious we were attracted to each other. She said she was going to get rid of Louie (I didn't ask how) so we could hang out together. Today, people call it hooking up but it meant the same thing. We went back to her apartment for a little up close and personal contact.

The world got smaller. Cindy lived on the same street as my soon-to-be ex-wife. Actually, she lived just a few houses away. I chuckled as I parked my car – the Lotus – in her driveway. That car was impossible to hide so I suspected there would be hell to pay the next day.

We walked around to the back of the house where the entrance to Cindy's apartment was located. In the northeast, it was not uncommon for a single family house to be converted into several apartments as rental property. Cindy lived in the basement; a couple lived upstairs. The two apartments were connected by an interior staircase and secured by a locked door.

Hours passed. We fell asleep and were awakened by Louie trying to get in. He had a key, but Cindy had put the chain on the door, and he was getting frustrated. He started yelling through the crack, "Cindy, you in there? Open the door."

We jumped out of bed. Cindy was freaking out. I dressed fast as she unlocked the door between the two apartments. I ran up the stairs as quietly as possible and let myself out the front door. As I was heading to my car, I heard Cindy and Louie fighting. A door slammed. Next thing I knew, Louie came from the back of the house. He was moving fast, but when he saw me, he slowed down and nodded. He still didn't recognize me and never suspected a thing. I got in my car and left. Oh… and my wife never knew either.

CHAPTER NINE

I've always been a nice guy. I wasn't always a good guy. If it's possible to be smart and stupid at the same time, that was the teenaged me. I made some stupid choices, but by some miracle, I never got into bad trouble. Maybe, I was just lucky. Luck, as you know, does not come in limitless supply. It tends to run out. In 2005, my pocketful of miracles got a hole in it, but before then...

I became an entrepreneur at the age of 19. Working at my dad's bakery and being well paid made it possible for me to help my buddies out when they needed cash. Most of them needed cash to buy drugs, which they resold. I would then get my investment back plus a vig. I also got all the drugs I wanted. That's a perfect example of being smart and stupid.

Louie the Italian sold drugs at the different nightclubs we frequented. He made a lot of money and he always paid his debts. In those days – my worst days – I drank a lot and did drugs, often doing both while driving. In case we got stopped by the cops, I would fill a glass Gatorade bottle with ice and Dewar's to hide the *evidence*. Louie and me... we could snort coke while behind the wheel. Our little fingers easily found their way to our nostrils.

There was only one problem. Louie just couldn't snort unless he was looking in a mirror. That's difficult to do in a car, especially if you're using the vanity mirror. On one particular night, the two of us were out on the town. I was drinking. Louie spent a lot of time staring at his nose in the glass. Out of the corner of my eye, I saw a cop car pull up beside us. There were two cops in the front and one in the back.

I yelled, "Cops! Don't turn your head. Just look straight in front of you."

While I was yelling, I saw the cop in the back seat point at us and say something to the other two. I was so engrossed in watching the cops that I didn't see the traffic light turn red and the cars in front of us come to a stop. I hit my brakes and skidded but, luckily, didn't hit anything. The cop driving the police car also hit his brakes, but he skidded into the car in front. That car was pushed into the intersections where it was hit by another car. It was frigging mayhem.

As soon as the light turned green, I took off. We drove through three lights before pulling into the back parking lot of one of our favorite clubs. A Lotus is not easy to hide, especially one with *World Champion 038* written on the side, but the back lot was dark, so I prayed my luck would hold out.

Louie and I lost track of the time. It was the wee hours of the morning when we left. No sooner did we get to the parking lot than we saw cop cars all over the place. We turned toe and went back inside. I knew that one of the girls who came to that club lived nearby. Her name was Rosemary. I asked her if she could drive a stick shift. She said "No," but she had a friend who could. Perfect. I gave Roe the keys and told her to drive my car to her house. In the meantime, Louie was freaking out because he had left a bag of coke in the car. I didn't share that bit of information with the girls.

We watched Roe and her friend from inside the club. They couldn't figure out how to start the car or put it in reverse. The engine was grinding. In desperation, they got out of the car and pushed it out of the parking space. No kidding. They pushed it out, got back in and drove away, all the while the car was bucking as they tried to switch gears. The cops stood there and watched.

Eventually, the cops realized that, maybe, they should follow the girls. One behind the other, like a line of ducklings following their mother, out of the parking lot they drove. But that's all they did. They never turned on their lights or sirens. They never tried to stop the girls. As an exit approached, one police car would pull off the highway. Louie and I were following in Roe's car and saw everything.

With the Lotus being on law enforcement's radar, I decided to trade it in and buy a Jaguar. Nicky invited me to a big party in Dix Hills. The guy who was hosting the party was loaded. The house was like a palace. There was a fountain in the middle of the driveway and parked on either side was a beautiful, brand new Excalibur.

Inside was even more beautiful than outside. There was an atrium with a jacuzzi and most of the guests were gathered there. Nicky introduced me to the owner, and he invited us up to his bedroom where he had a huge stash of coke. We took what we wanted and went back to the party.

I met a girl and in short time she and I decided to leave. We went to a hotel. We had a good time together, but it was a one night affair. I never saw her again. Four days after the party, Nicky called me. "Rosario, you're not going to believe this. Somebody killed the guy who had the party. They have our faces on the surveillance tape."

Nicky and I went to the police station to give a statement, but thanks to the cameras outside the house, I was in the clear. The cops saw me leave early with the girl. She and I were each other's alibis – not that we needed any.

The world is now getting smaller. I used to deliver bread in Freeport for my dad. It was my habit to put "Paid" or "Unpaid" on the bills so my sister, who did the bookkeeping, would know what was collected and what wasn't. My handwriting sucked and, often, she couldn't tell what I had written. To make her life easier, she bought me a pen with a *Paid* stamp on one end. I had it only a few days when I lost it.

Not wanting my sister to kill me, I started to call all the places where I had made deliveries. One of them was The Tides. I spoke to someone who spoke to someone and, eventually, a girl got on the phone who said she had the pen. But… she said I had to prove the pen was mine. She was flirting with me and I was happy to go along with it. To get the pen, she wanted me to come to her house and bring champagne and orange juice to make mimosas.

One thing led to another and when the important stuff was done, she took out a photograph album. Now, I have to tell you that this girl had a rock on her finger the size of a baseball, but she would never tell me who had given it to her. Anyway, we're looking through the album and what did I see but the house where the guy was killed. There's the fountain and the cars… just the way I remembered it. Turned out, she had been his fiancé. She was at the party the night I was there, but we never saw each other. She claimed not to know any details about the murder. I thought it best not to make a second date.

CHAPTER TEN

When I first started delivering for my dad's bakery, I was still in my teens. I had been driving for years, even without a license, so I knew how to handle a truck. The hours were long; delivery guys are awake when most other people are asleep. We're like bats; we know our routes so well we could drive them with our eyes closed.

The job did have its perks. Life after my divorce wasn't much different than life before the split with Barbara. My routine was to load the truck around 11:00 pm, but before I could do that, I had to make up the orders for our customers. We had what we called *fast drop* bags, labeled so that we could be in and out quickly. A typical order was five dozen rolls and 50 heroes to a box.

Once all that was done, I changed my clothes and went to the clubs to party for a few hours. Without fail, I would meet a girl willing to go on my route with me. We would make the deliveries, have sex in the truck and then go to breakfast. Nice work if you can get it.

Every morning, near the end of my route, I passed a deli located in a strip mall. It was owned by a German man who had a thriving business.

Hungry and needing to stay awake, I would stop to buy food,

usually a bagel with cream cheese and jelly and a Yoohoo. There were a lot of people working even at that early hour.

It was natural for me to take note of what our competitors were offering, and it was usually inferior quality breads. I began bringing the deli owner a few of our best products... six seeded heroes and six poppy seed rolls. No charge. The bread was always fresh from the oven.

The guys working behind the counter knew I was trying to get their business. They liked me, so they told me that their current supplier had had the account for 15 years. There was little to no chance of taking it away from them. However, the manager of the deli department told me that, while the owner was happy enough with their supplier, he ate his sandwiches on my bread. That gave me an idea.

One morning when I went to pay for my breakfast, the owner said, "No charge." I respected that. He was repaying me for bringing him our bread every day. I took the opportunity to talk to him about giving us a try. He said, "No." I said, "Okay. Thanks anyway."

Even though the owner was not receptive to my offer, I continued to bring him the freebies every morning. Since I always got to the deli about the same time as the deli's regular delivery guy, I pretty much knew his routine. I bided my time, waiting for the day when he would drop his order and leave quickly. That would be my chance to up our odds of getting the account.

It was common practice for the delivery guy to leave the order outside the side door. As soon as he was out of sight, I stole all the bread. I had to move quickly not to get caught. Most of it I threw into the dumpsters behind a nearby Waldbaum's, but a few pieces I kept as samples to show my father. I also held onto the receipt which was with the order so that I would have a competitive edge in pricing.

After tossing the day's delivery in the trash, I went back inside the deli and ordered breakfast as usual. The owner was all upset because he thought his delivery guy had never made his stop. I told him I'd help him out; gave him all the bread I had left on my truck.

The next day I again waited for the delivery guy to leave so that I could swap out some of the fresh bread with the few sample pieces that

I had kept the day before. These were now a little stale, which didn't sit well with the owner.

Again, I went inside to get breakfast. The owner called me over. He said, "From now on, every day, I want you to bring me six dozen rolls and six dozen heroes."

Two months went by before I saw the other driver. He accused me of stealing his account but, truthfully, I didn't do anything different from what people had done to me many times over the years. Bread stealing was part of the job description.

Anyway, I delivered the same six dozen rolls and heroes to the German guy for years. Eventually, I got his entire order.

Some of our most lucrative customers were the local farm stands. To facilitate delivery, I took the empty banana boxes and used them to hold the fresh loaves of Italian bread. At the bakery, I loaded the boxes with each customer's order and when I got to the farm, I merely removed the empty boxes and replaced them with the full boxes. The boxes were turned on their side so customers could easily reach for a loaf or two.

Janet's Farm Stand in Nassau County was one of our best customers. It was owned by a guy named Chipper. Chipper also owned the Tides Restaurant in Freeport. He was a big connected guy… old school… tough. Janet was his girlfriend.

The farm stand made a fortune mostly because the milk was so cheap. Chipper sold it way below cost. Business was booming, and we sold a lot of bread there. In fact, we were selling so much bread that my dad hired a carpenter to build a special display rack.

I'm sure you know that when you buy a loaf of Italian bread in a waxed paper bag, one side of the bag is open and the end of the loaf is visible. In Nassau county, when the bread is put on a shelf, the visible end has to be facing toward the wall… away from the customer. A crazy rule, but one we had to follow.

Chipper was doing so well with Janet's that he opened a new place in Suffolk County. In Suffolk County, the bread on the shelf could be facing in or out. It got confusing sometimes, especially for new delivery guys.

Again, the new farm stand made money hand over fist, and my dad hired the same carpenter to build another shelf for our bread. There were traffic jams in the street every day all day long. One day, I was filling the shelves with fresh bread and a big guy I'd never seen before approached me. I didn't know he was one of Chipper's partners.

This guy was a nasty piece of work. He called me a "stupid bastard" and told me to put the bread on the shelf facing toward the wall. I tried to explain to him that Suffolk County did not follow the same guidelines as Nassau County, but he wouldn't listen. No matter how many times I tried to explain, he cut me off. I was getting angry and he was spoiling for a fight.

He screamed, "Take the fucking bread out of here," and kicked a box, scattering the loaves across the floor. The customers froze where they were standing. I said, "You kicked the box, you pick up the bread," and I walked out. The guy gathered up the boxes and loaves of bread and threw them out into the parking lot. I drove away. Of course, my dad lost both farm stand accounts.

By the time I got back to the bakery, my dad had heard what happened and he was furious. We lost a lot of money that day. My father made me go back and apologize. All was forgiven, but I wasn't allowed to deliver to either store. And... despite the Suffolk County guidelines, we had to put the bread on the shelves facing in just like in Nassau County.

A year passed and my dad had no one to make the delivery so he sent me. When I arrived, the nasty guy wasn't around, but as I was loading the shelves, he came in. He walked up to me and said, "You're that little wise ass." I said, "Listen, I'm just doing my job." He laughed, "I gotta admit, you got balls." After that, we were okay with each other.

CHAPTER ELEVEN

At first, Dad just made bread. He had 14 trucks and was making a good living, but the work was exhausting. One day, he was approached by a major competitor – Augie's Bakery. Augie grew his business by buying other bakeries, but he wasn't very smart. He bought my father out but within two years, Augie went bust.

Dad had fortunately only sold his routes, so he still had all his property and the building. Unfortunately, he had already sold or given away his equipment, making it too late to get back in the bread baking business.

Luck was on our side. One of my father's regular customers was a guy named Joel. Joel had a bread delivery business in Manhattan. While on his route, he learned of another guy who was making a cracker that had become a hot item. He brought my dad a sample and asked if Dad could make them. My father said, "Yeah. No problem."

So, Dad made the crackers. Joel loved them. The crackers were hand cut and packaged in plastic bags. Dad and Joel called them Sunshine Flats.

Making the crackers was easy, but hand cutting them into serving sized pieces was tedious. Dad eventually got a machine that sliced the crackers into large gourmet squares. The process then became semi-automated, but it was expensive and required raising the price of the crackers to cover the overhead.

Since Dad had sold his route to Augie, we had to build the cracker business from the ground up. By this time, I was in my twenties. I started by pitching Sunshine Flats at our local Waldbaum store. Once I had that account secured, I asked for directions to the next closest Waldbaum's. I went from location to location and within a very short time signed up 140 stores.

Irwin Hartman, the then executive in charge of purchasing for Waldbaum's, and I became friends. He knew a good seller when he saw it – the crackers, not me - and because he was confident that our company would always supply a quality product, he was happy to become our first large distributor. When Waldbaum's was bought out by A&P, I saw it as icing on the Sunshine Flats.

I did the same thing with the D'Agastino chain, which was a family-owned supermarket operating in New York City. Sunshine Flats was on its way to becoming a staple in homes and restaurants.

So far, I've just given you the straight up side of doing business in New York, but there was a lot going on behind the scenes. After selling the bread route to Augie, Dad bought bagel equipment from a guy named Brownie. Brownie invited Dad to a party at his house where he met Paul. You've probably noticed that very few of these people have last names. It's not that I have a bad memory. It's just better that way.

Paul was a good-looking guy. Reminded me of Don Johnson – expensive clothing, drove a Porsche, always had a gorgeous woman on his arm. He oversaw the deli departments for all the A&P Supermarkets.

How many of you remember A&P? Do you know what A&P stands for? I didn't until I was much older. The Great Atlantic and Pacific Tea Company. What a mouthful! Their headquarters were in Montvale, New Jersey, and when they closed in 2015, they had been in business for 156 years.

Anyway, Dad introduced me to Paul, and we immediately hit it off. Just friends but with the potential for a lucrative future.

About this same time, Dad had a distribution deal with John Englishman, who was a broker for food products. Food brokers are independent sales agents who negotiate deals between food producers - like bakers - and buyers - like A&P. Just keep that in mind for now.

CHAPTER TWELVE

I was making good money working for my dad. I loved cars and, back then, I bought a lot of them. I owned a 1962 Oldsmobile F-85, a 1967 Ford Galaxy, and a 428 Cobra Jet. These cars I bought second hand. Then, I got a 1975 Cougar XR7, my first brand new car. After that, I bought a gorgeous burgundy Corvette, which I had customized to the tune of an extra $10,000. I gave the Cougar to my brother Anthony, who had just gotten his license.

One day, while I was making a delivery to Pastosa Ravioli on Deer Park Avenue, a car making a weird noise pulled up beside my truck. The driver, a kind of hippie looking guy, went into the store. I waited for him to come out.

When he did, I asked him what kind of a car he was driving. He said, "A Lotus Esprit." More conversation and he told me he bought it at Sportique Motors in Huntington, Long Island. I said, "Thanks," and the guy left. Now, I wanted to own a Lotus.

The owner of Pastosa told me that the guy with the fancy car was the guitarist for the rock group, Foreigner, and that he lived in Dix Hills, a ritzy section of Long Island.

I was married to my first wife, Barbara, at the time, and she didn't think we needed another car. She used to drive our Corvette to work. I had the truck. Barbara felt that was good enough. I didn't.

Without telling her, I drove the vette to Sportique and parked it out front. I was dressed like a laborer; not the kind of person who could afford an expensive car. When I walked into the showroom, the salesmen looked at me like I was going to rob the place. After an exchange of eye rolls, the manager walked over.

I told him I was interested in buying the white Lotus that was displayed on the floor. He said, "No way."

From the condescending tone of his voice, it was obvious that "No way" meant "Who are you kidding." He blew me off; turned me over to another salesman by the name of Larry.

Larry didn't look too thrilled to talk to me either. Like his boss, he thought owning a Lotus was out of my league. When I told Larry how much I liked the car on the floor, he said that it was already sold. I said I could wait; told him to let me know when another car came in. Then, I pointed to my Vette parked at the curb.

Suddenly, all the other salesmen who had avoided me when I first entered the dealership couldn't wait to shake my hand. We began to talk business. I told Larry I wanted to trade in the Corvette, and they tried to low ball me on the price as I knew they would. We went back and forth until I got what I wanted for my car.

The next step was to find an available Lotus that I liked. They showed me a photo of a black and gold one – the same car owned by Mario Andretti. It was perfect.

Mario Andretti's car was #001. My car was #038 to roll off the assembly line. Both cars were manufactured by Rolls Royce. Mine set me back $27,000.

Man, did I ever love that car. Sometimes I think my life would have been simpler if cars, rather than women, had been my true passion.

My buddies were excited about the Lotus, but my father wanted to kill me; mostly because I had bought it from a photograph. The car I chose was in California and would take three weeks to arrive. It needed to be sent via cargo ship to the Port of New York.

When it arrived, Larry sent someone to pick it up at the pier. I was standing in the showroom when the driver pulled up. I heard the crunch as he turned into the dealership, steering the car over high ground and crushing the bottom in the process. Antifreeze was everywhere.

Larry told me not to worry. He said they would make it "brand new again," but it would take a few weeks as parts had to come from London. In the meantime, they gave me a new Peugeot to drive as they had already found a buyer for my Corvette.

By the time the Lotus was ready, the trade in value on the Vette had dropped $3,000. I was angry and told Larry to forget the deal; they could keep the Lotus. The manager heard us arguing and, immediately, told Larry to make the deal as originally agreed. I drove away a happy man!

That car got me in a lot of trouble as you will learn later in this story so, maybe, women were a better passion after all.

When my daughter, Erica, was born in 1984, I traded the Lotus for a 1984 Jaguar HE Sport. It was a two door, four-seater, 12- cylinder sports model.

True story about the Jaguar. The day I bought my car, Billy Joel was at the dealership buying the same car. I'm assuming you know

who Billy Joel is since he's much more famous than A&P. The Jag Billy ordered was green. Mine was gold. We talked. He was a nice guy and, obviously, had great taste in cars... and women. I admired him.

I ran into Billy a few times after that, mostly at the Toys for Tots Motorcycle Run hosted annually by the Marines. Whenever he saw me, he always friendly. Like I said, he was a nice guy.

One Friday night in early May, my buddies and I decided to take a few hot girls to Atlantic City. We were heading into one of the casinos when who came out – Paul. He saw me and said, "Holy shit! What're you doing here?"

I made introductions all around, and we headed inside. Paul bought drinks for everybody. I'd like to think he was impressed by me but, mostly, he couldn't take his eyes off the ladies.

The conversation eventually came around to A&P buying Waldbaum's. I told Paul that Waldbaum's had been carrying our Sunshine Flats crackers for years and that they were a big seller. He asked me to send him samples and gave me a phone number to call to set up an appointment. I was juiced.

As soon as I got home, I called my father to tell him the good news, but he wasn't feeling the excitement. Dad was always a worrier, and now he was worried that we couldn't handle the volume. A&P had 1200 stores. Just the thought of having to meet that demand nearly gave him a stroke.

Any deal we made with A&P would put us on the gravy train for the rest of our lives. I wasn't about to give up. I convinced Dad to take the appointment with Paul by saying we didn't have to supply all the A&P stores. We could start with 100 or so.

It took a lot of talking which, thankfully, I'm good at. Dad finally agreed to go to the meeting with Paul. He wanted to take John Englishman for funding purposes, but I convinced him otherwise. I was concerned we would appear overly confident, and I really thought we were just going there to pitch our product. Plus, I cockily thought my friendship with Paul would be all that was needed to clinch the deal. Talk about naive.

Dad and I drove to New Jersey for the meeting. Who should I see when we get there? John Englishman. I was stunned. Without telling me, my dad had invited him to the meeting.

I was pissed but not as pissed as Paul, who immediately demanded to know why Englishman was present. I didn't have an answer. Paul looked me in the eyes and said, "No meeting."

We never got the A&P account.

CHAPTER THIRTEEN

I always had the feeling that Paul knew Englishman from some other business deal, but neither of them ever admitted to anything. Anyway, getting that account would have been great. Instead of having to deliver to individual stores, we would have made one drop at a warehouse, and A&P would have done the distribution themselves.

My father and I argued all the way home to Babylon; it was the beginning of the end of our working relationship. The loss of that deal hit me hard. I no longer cared about the bakery; I began drinking and partying, staying out late and doing coke. I still went to work every day, but I was furious with my father. Whenever a non-corporate account paid in cash, I kept the money. Partying all night was expensive.

While I loved my Jaguar, I really wanted something bigger. I decided to give my mom and dad the Jag and get myself a Bronco, which I bought through the business. This was also about the time my father, a former marine, was reaching his limit with my attitude. Much to my shame, I must admit to being damned disrespectful, and Dad wasn't going to take it anymore. We argued constantly about my partying and pocketing of company money.

There came a day when we got into a huge fight in front of the bakery. I jumped into the Bronco intent on leaving, but the keys were gone. I knew my father had taken them, and I started yelling at him to give them to me. I started "yelling" is an understatement. When I'm angry, the whole world knows it.

Dad stared me down; said the truck belonged to him because it was bought with company money. I was beyond crazy. I got a hammer from the back and tried to smash the distributor cap. Dad put me in a chokehold.

Remember, I told you he was a former Marine. Yeah. Well, Marines are never "former" anything. The chokehold worked. We both fell to the ground, and I stopped fighting back.

Once I caught my breath, I stood up, turned my back on my father and walked away from the bakery, never looking behind me. Man, did I ever learn the meaning of hindsight that day.

I hoofed it to my new girlfriend's house. She also had a Bronco – smaller than mine – and she let me drive it while I looked for a job. Within a few days, I was employed at a Greek deli in Freeport. I hated it!

Adding to my misery, the divorce from my second wife wasn't going well. When I moved out, I gave Kim our Trans Am. I also sent her money every month to pay the car loan.

I knew nothing about her failure to make payments until I got a call from my dad, who had taken a call from GMC at the bakery. When I finally talked to the agent, he told me that I was three months behind in my payments, and they were going to repossess the car. Smoke was coming out of my ears!

Kim claimed she needed the money for herself and our two kids. In fact, she wanted even more money -- $400 more a month. Fuel for the fire!

Wanting to teach her a lesson, I called the agent at GMC and asked if I could still get the car towed even if I made all the delinquent payments. He thought I was nuts but said if I paid the tow truck driver, I could do whatever I wanted. So, I made the payments and had the car towed from the driveway of the house Kim and I owned. Now, she didn't have any car.

Eventually, I went and picked up the car and brought it back to my apartment. It was always my intention to give it back to Kim in the divorce settlement. I really wanted her and our kids to be happy, and I was willing to give them whatever they wanted.

Being employed at the Greek deli didn't help my state of mind. I was still drinking heavily. My new girlfriend broke up with me and that made me drink even more. I was a mess all because of that lost deal with A&P. What a jerk I was!

Eventually, I quit the Greek place and took a job with one of my Dad's competitors, Modern Bakery. Modern hired me as a salesman knowing I would increase their business, but my reading and writing skills were lacking. Filling out the required paperwork was almost enough to drive me over the edge.

Every day, after loading my truck with Modern Bakery's products, I would head over to Dad's warehouse and pick up a supply of Sunshine Crackers. I drove all over… to Montauk and the Hamptons trying to build up my route. In case you're wondering, Montauk is not officially a part of the Hamptons, although it lies on the East End of Long Island.

A few months passed, and I was doing pretty good. Then, I learned that my uncle - my father's sister's husband – had died. Aunt Jeannie and Uncle Dominic lived in Florida, where they owned a drywall company.

Dad and I were on good terms by then, but I wouldn't have blamed him if he never spoke to me again. My old man has a forgiving soul for which I am very grateful. He encouraged me to go to Florida and help my cousin run the business. He said it would be a new start for me and, just like when he tried to tell me to stop partying and drugging, he was right.

Housing wasn't going to be a problem because Aunt Jeannie had a room for me. However, she didn't have a television, and I knew I was going to need one to unwind at the end of the day. So, my clothes went into my suitcase and my television went into a box. To be honest, it was Dad who told me to take the TV. The man always knew me better than I knew myself.

Dad insisted on taking me to the airport. Leaving the bakery even for only a few hours cost him more than just production time. It cost him money as well. He was struggling with the bakery because he now had to pay a lot of people to do the work I used to do by myself. I felt like a heel.

We drove along the Sunrise Highway, and we were both crying. We couldn't talk, and we wouldn't look at each other. I got to thinking "What if I never see him again." Despite what happened between us, I love my Dad more than anyone or anything. We're very close now.

When we got to the airport, I put the tv and my suitcase in cargo, gave my dad a long hug and walked away. Three and half hours later, I landed in Florida.

CHAPTER FOURTEEN

My second marriage ended for pretty much the same reasons as the first. The two best things to come out of those years are my kids, whom I adore.

After I moved to Florida, I would go home every month, so I could spend time with my son and daughter. My normal routine was to fly Eastern Airlines out of Fort Lauderdale, landing in West Islip, where my dad would pick me up. I spent my afternoons with Erica and Jimmy doing whatever made them happy. I really missed not seeing them every day.

Traveling in the winter was the hardest. Snowstorms often pummeled the northeast, delaying flights for hours. Most passengers spent the time drinking at a bar near the departure gate. You know me… I've got a million stories, so I took it upon myself to keep everybody entertained. On one trip, a woman walked into the bar, and the storm Mother Nature was raging in New York was nothing compared to what I felt looking at her. Her name was Denise, and she was about to change my life forever.

Denise looked like the actress Vanessa Williams, and she was dressed like she had just stepped out of the pages of a fashion magazine. She had the most unusual yellow eyes. Yellow eyes! I had never seen eyes like hers before… or since.

To make the situation even stranger, she was carrying two bags of garlic crabs. Just imagine. A drop dead gorgeous woman, wearing an expensive fur coat and jewels and carrying bags of garlic crabs. The picture she made was beyond weird… and wonderful.

Since this happened long before 9/11, family and friends could escort passengers to their departure gate. Denise was with a much older man, and they seemed very affectionate toward each other. I couldn't help but notice the Rock of Gibraltar on the ring finger of her left hand. The man eventually left, and Denise stood alone looking for a place to sit. Being a gentleman, I jumped up and offered her my seat. She didn't want to take it, but I insisted. She said "Okay," but only if she could buy me a drink. We had a deal. Another guy joined us and the three of us drank for almost 90 minutes before our flight was called.

By then, I was buzzed and completely entranced by this stranger. Denise was also having a grand old time. I lost track of how many times she expressed the wish that we could sit together on the plane. I told her, "Just follow my lead."

When our flight was called, I took her by the arm and walked up to the ticket counter. With a twinkle in my eyes, I said to the agent, "Listen. What kind of an airline is this? We just got engaged, and we couldn't get a seat together. You are interfering with the course of true love." I held up Denise's hand to show the agent her ring.

I felt a little guilty for lying; the agent was so apologetic. She promised to see what she could do, but the plane was full, and she didn't think any passengers would be willing to change seats. We boarded the plane and went our separate ways. Denise was in the front and I was way in the back.

When we got on the plane, the pilot was standing at the door greeting everyone. I started to tell him *our* story. Jokingly, I said, "Boy, some company you are. I should have taken Delta." Everybody was laughing.

The plane began to taxi down the runway. Denise was so far in the front that I couldn't see her. I noticed the attendant motion for a passenger to follow her to first class. When she stood up, I could see her coat. It was Denise. Then, the attendant walked back to me and brought me to first class. We rode to New York in style, celebrating our engagement the whole way.

As we waited for our luggage at the baggage terminal, Denise gave me her parents' phone number and asked if we could get together later that night. Come on. Do I really have to tell you my answer?

With the phone number safely secured in my wallet, we said "Goodbye." Denise left with her mom and dad, and I left with my father. Later that night, we went out on the town. Most nights, after my kids were safely tucked into bed, were spent together... all platonic. It was the perfect trip. During the day, I had my kids, who I loved with all my heart, and at night I had Denise, who I was beginning to love in the same way.

Back in Florida, three weeks passed, but despite Denise's promise to call me, the phone never rang. I had just about given up hope when she contacted me. We made plans to meet at Bennigan's. I took off from work – at the time, I was working as a bouncer at a local club -- just so I could spend time with her. We started dating, but I was conflicted. She was still living with her fiancé, and I wasn't looking for trouble.

One night after work, I decided to grab a bite to eat with one of the waitresses before going home. She and I were friends, nothing more. When you work nights, it's hard to unwind at the end of a shift. Going out to eat is a common practice.

We left the club and got into my car. Suddenly, there was a tap on the window. Denise was standing beside the car looking in at me. I could see she had gotten the wrong impression; she started to berate me, accusing me of cheating on her. I wasn't, and even if I was having another relationship, Denise and I had never made a commitment to each other. How could we? She was sleeping with her finance every night while I went home alone. After an exchange of words, she told me she was moving out, which she did. We quickly moved in together.

After we became an item, Denise took control of my life in a good way. She made sure that I rectified all the mistakes I had made in New

York (there had been a few brushes with the law in my youth). She also took over all the bookkeeping for Rosario's Flatbread Crackers and had the office running smoothly. This happened before my cousin Dom and his wife Valerie began handling the administrative side of the business.

Denise and I were together for five years. Although we were never officially engaged, I've always thought of her as a wife. I cared about her a lot.

CHAPTER FIFTEEN

I worked hard my whole life, and it all went to shit in about two seconds. Even now, after the trial and prison, I don't really know what happened. The media... they painted me as a mobster but, although I knew some of those guys (in the food industry, it's a given that you will meet and do business with members of organized crime), I was not one of them. I don't want my children to think that what was printed in the newspapers was true; I don't want them ashamed of me or their last name.

Because of what happened, I wasn't there for my kids when they needed me. I know I'm not the only guy to be railroaded by the system. There are a lot of us; I'm not making excuses or blame-shifting. I went to trial thinking justice would be served. It wasn't. I did my time.

∼

Prison is 24 hours of boredom followed by 24 more hours of boredom day after day. It's even worse when you've been convicted of a crime you didn't commit.

I was desperate to break the monotony, so I started painting pictures for my son. On visitors' day, my wife Sheryl would take the paintings home, but I wasn't allowed to give them to her.

Prisoners were not permitted to exchange anything with their family and friends... not coming in and not going out. Nothing ever changed hands.

For Sheryl to take the pictures out of the prison, I had to log them in at the property room, which was in the medical building -- a long distance from the main part of the jail. Inmates did not need a pass to go to the prop room. Once the paintings were logged in, I was given a receipt. Sheryl could then claim them when she left.

When Sheryl and I got married in 2001, we had a Mercedes SL and a Navigator. Sheryl mostly drove the Mercedes while I drove the Navigator for business. We were only married a few months when she had a terrible accident.

I got a call from the police telling me that she had been taken to Delray Medical Center. When I arrived there, I almost didn't recognize her. She was wrapped in bandages and had a breathing tube in her mouth. There was also a feeding tube in her stomach. The doctor told me she was in an induced coma. They didn't think she would survive.

I had barely adjusted to what I was seeing when a different doctor asked if I would donate her organs. It was like being in the ring with Mohammed Ali and getting punched... a fist to the gut over and over again. Every word that came out of the doctor's mouth destroyed any hope for her recovery. I refused to accept the prognosis.

Sheryl's mother had been traveling extensively, so we had never met. Imagine hugging your new mother-in-law while standing at the side of her daughter's bed waiting for her to die. I wasn't going to let that happen. We took turns staying at the hospital. Sheryl's mom was there during the day, and I took the night shift.

I don't know if it was the excellent care Sheryl received from us or if God decided it wasn't her time, but every day she got a little better. Weeks passed, and she began breathing on her own... not all on her own… but enough that she was less reliant on the machines. When the nurse told me that the tubes were going to be removed, it was like Christmas morning. Sheryl still wasn't Sheryl, but now I truly believed there was a chance she would get better.

One night when I walked into her room, I saw that the tubes were gone, but Sheryl's head was tilted in an unnatural position. It was bent toward one shoulder as if her neck had been broken and left to heal without straightening. Her face was contorted, too. The nurse told me it often happened when a patient had been on a breathing machine for a long time because the muscles contract and freeze in place.

I couldn't stand to see Sheryl like that. It looked painful, so I asked the nurse for whatever cream was available and began massaging Sheryl's neck. I did it for hours. It took three days but, eventually, she was able to move her head again. I remember the first night the nurse came in to check on Sheryl and saw me massaging her. She said, "I want one just like you at home."

It made me feel good to know I was doing the right things. The nurses were very accommodating. They let me stay in the room all night. I slept in a chair next to Sheryl and held her hand. Each day, I took on more of the nurses' duties. They were so overworked, and I was happy to be doing something.

I even learned how to give Sheryl a manicure. She had fake nails… acrylics… which began to grow a fungus. I wanted to hire a manicurist to remove them, but the hospital wouldn't allow it. So, I went to Sheryl's regular salon and had the nail tech teach me what to do. I soaked the acrylics off, trimmed and buffed her nails, cut her cuticles… no more fungus.

In the three months Sheryl was hospitalized, I saw some terrible tragedies. I don't want to recount them all here, but I learned to be grateful for small miracles. As bad as Sheryl's injuries were, she had a chance to live a normal life. Being in the hospital for so long, I got an education I wish I hadn't needed. Trauma doctors and nurses are very special people. They don't get the credit they deserve. Every day, they save lives. They work miracles.

There were three construction workers who fell 40 feet from a roof.

They all broke their backs. Two of them were paralyzed and couldn't speak. The third guy could talk; his injuries didn't seem as severe, but he was the one who died. It was crazy.

I learned to lift Sheryl from the bed to a wheelchair. I would give her a shower, wash and dry her hair, brush it until it was shiny, dress her... all the things that the nurses would have had to do, but I knew Sheryl would be happier with me doing it. There wasn't anything I wouldn't have done for her.

When she was moved to a private room, I was able to sleep in the bed with her. By now, she knew I was there and while she still couldn't talk, she could communicate in other ways. The injuries to her head made thinking and speaking difficult. It was so frightening to see Sheryl struggle to remember small details that had been a part of her daily life. Looking at her, you could see the battle she was fighting to get better. The frustration drove her crazy.

The feeding tube had been in so long that Sheryl forgot how to eat. Her gag reflex was working overtime and she couldn't swallow. Those feeding tubes... I don't know what kind of concoction patients are given, but I fed her some disgusting looking green stuff. As I said earlier, I learned a lot while Sheryl was in the hospital. I never knew that even though a patient is fed through a feeding tube in their stomach, if they get nauseated, they vomit through their mouth. I was so careful to do the feeding slowly, so she didn't feel sick. I kept promising her that as soon as she was better, I would cook all her favorite foods.

The doctor told me that many of Sheryl's problems were being caused by fluid on the brain. He needed to put a shunt in her skull. She had beautiful hair, and she was proud of it. When the doctor told me what he was going to do, I asked if he had to shave Sheryl's head. He said he would try not to do that. The next night when I got to the hospital, she was bald. My heart sunk because I knew how upset she would be.

As devastating as the hair loss was, the shunt changed everything. Sheryl was awake, alert and trying to speak. When she saw me, she tried to say "Hi." It was just a sound, not a word, but she was talking.

She could nod her head "yes" and "no" and her face was animated again.

More improvements came from physical therapy. She had to be taught how to use her hands, how to sit and walk, And, of course, how to eat. She had lost so much weight, the scale registered 80 pounds. Once she could stand without falling, the nurses would tie a karate belt around her waist. I would hold onto it from the back, and we would walk up and down the hall ways, so she could get exercise and strengthen her muscles.

One of the best nights was when I arrived to find the feeding tube had been removed. My mother-in-law was sitting next to the bed and said to Sheryl, "Tell Rosario what you ate today." I was elated. I kept saying to her, "Tell me. Tell me."

Sheryl pointed down to the floor meaning she and her mom had gone to the cafeteria. I asked, "What did you get? A hamburger?" She shook her head "No" and said "Opposite." She was telling me she had eaten a hot dog. Getting her thoughts together was still a problem.

When Sheryl was able to go home, it was one of the happiest days of our lives. Since she had lost so much weight, none of her clothes fit. We went shopping. She was so excited to feel human again. I remember she wanted to buy clogs. I was a little leery about the heels because while she could walk, she wasn't completely steady on her feet. I should have listened to my gut.

Sheryl put the shoes on to go home, and she was okay while I was holding on to her. On the way back, we stopped at the bakery, so I could handle some business. I told Sheryl to stay in the Navigator, but the minute I was out of sight, she tried to get out. She fell and hit the ground so hard, I heard her head hit the pavement. She was knocked out.

I can't remember ever moving that fast before or since. Back in the car, I drove like a madman to the hospital. Four hours of testing and, thankfully, she was okay. After that, I was afraid to leave her alone. If not for my mother-in-law, I don't know what I would have done. I needed to work a few hours a day, and then there were all the therapies

Sheryl still needed... physical therapy, speech therapy... it went on and on.

Just when we thought everything was going well, we faced another problem. While Sheryl was taking a bath, I noticed that one of her breasts was normal while the other one was swollen and discolored. I'm not talking a little swollen. It was close to rivaling a basketball. When I touched it, it burned against my fingers. I rushed her back to the hospital.

The doctors took x-rays and saw that the shunt in her head had been dislodged when she fell. I never knew how a shunt worked, so the doctor explained the procedure for me. He told me that the surgeon had made a tiny incision behind Sheryl's ear and then drilled a small hole in her skull. A catheter was threaded into the brain through the opening. Another catheter went behind her ear just under the skin. The tube ran down the chest and into the abdomen, allowing excess brain fluid to drain into the abdominal cavity so the body could absorb it. Instead of draining into Sheryl's stomach, the fluid was going into her breast. The doctor did another surgery to correct the problem, and it went well, but that was so scary. I'll never forget it.

All that happened nearly 20 years ago. The woman the doctors thought would not survive is doing all the things she did before the accident. Occasionally, she struggles to find a word or to express a thought, but we all do that. The only lingering side effect is that she lost her sense of smell. When I come home from a long day at work, and she gives me a hug, I tease her that she can only do that because she can't smell me.

Sheryl got pregnant with Rosario, Jr. a few months after leaving the hospital. We felt blessed. She needed help taking care of him, but again, her mom came to the rescue. I don't know what I would have done without her.

Twelve years in prison changes a man. When I got home, it was difficult for me to be intimate with Sheryl. Plus, I'm older, and Sheryl is still a young woman. We're working through our problems, and everyday our smiles get bigger. I love my wife and my children. Nothing is going to stop me from making a happy life for all of us.

Thinking back over Sheryl's accident and my time in prison, I realize that no matter the difficulties fate has put in my path, I am a lucky man.

∽

I asked Sheryl if she would write how she felt hearing the verdict at the trial. This is what she told me.

"When the verdict was read, my heart broke. My husband… the man I loved… the man who had cared for me during the most difficult time of my life… was going away for a long time. I couldn't image what I would do without him, especially with having to care for Rosario, Jr., who was only one year old.

Ever since the car accident, Rosario had been my strength. When Rosario, Jr. was born, he spent less time at work, so he could help me at home. He always took care of us.

After the trial, I was suddenly alone and didn't know how to do anything for myself. The mere thought of being without Rosario to lean on crushed me, especially at night. After he was permanently incarcerated, my mom had to come to live with me, so she could help with the baby.

Even now, with Rosario home, the adjustment is difficult. I'm afraid to let him out of my sight. Afraid he won't come back… that someone will harm him, or there will be a car accident, or he will get hurt at work. My mind is filled with scary thoughts and, even though I know they are unreasonable, I can't stop them."

~ Sheryl Liotta ~

CHAPTER SIXTEEN

Visitation rules are strictly enforced in prison. Each inmate is limited to five adult visitors at any visit. Inmates must be dressed in their Class A uniform, which includes a blue shirt tucked into blue pants and proper shoes. The rules specifically stress the need to put on underclothing and socks. The underwear rule is due to the lack of intimacy allowed between prisoners and their wives or girlfriends. You would be amazed at how clever couples can be in securing "private" time together. Inmates are strip searched before entering the visitors room and after exiting.

As I've already said, for inmates to send anything home with a visitor, arrangements had to be made with the property room clerk the Wednesday before the visiting weekend.

One day, the line at the prop room was long, maybe eight or nine people ahead of me. A guy I knew told me my name was being called from the loud speakers. Once I had my receipt, I went outside and spoke to the guard standing at the fence. "I'm Liotta. I heard somebody is looking for me?"

He growled. "Turn around. You're in deep shit." Then, he grabbed his cuffs, slapped them on my wrists, and dragged me to the control room.

I had no idea what was happening. When we got to the control room, both the warden and the security warden were waiting. They looked like deer caught in a car's headlights. Seems they had been searching for me for two hours and thought I was AWOL.

Suddenly, two new guys came into the room. One guy was about six and a half feet tall; the other guy was short with a very noticeable toupee. He was respectful toward me. Said, "Mr. Liotta, we're here to talk to you."

They hadn't introduced themselves, so I was hesitant to say anything. The short guy handed me a business card:

Organized Crime Unit
FBI Homicide Division
New York City

Trust me. If you're in prison, you don't ever want to get a card like that. When the Feds come calling, it's nothing but trouble.

The big guy tried his best to intimidate me. "We've got your ass. This is about your victim. We're investigating murders that your victim committed."

I refused to engage with them. Merely said, "You gotta talk to my lawyer."

That's when they claimed my lawyer had sent them, but I knew that couldn't be true. My lawyer would have told me; he would have been there. I challenged them. "You have a phone. Call Duncan. If he says to talk to you, I'll talk to you."

At this point, things got interesting. The tall guy told me that it wasn't Douglas Duncan, my appeals lawyer, who sent them but David Bogenschutz, my trial lawyer. I was confused because Bogenschutz was no longer on the case.

We began to bicker; the tall guy got a little more threatening.

"We're here now and we're going to talk to you."

I was quiet... didn't want anything to do with them. If the other prisoners knew I was talking to the Feds, the story would be completely blown out of proportion.

Finally, I turned to the warden, "You know what? Lock me up because I ain't talking to these guys. Take me outta here." Then, to them, I said, "It was nice knowing you."

A guard took me away. The warden and security warden followed us out. The security warden tried to scare me into cooperating. "We're gonna lock you up in the box."

The box was a small two-man cell with barely enough room for the beds and a toilet. Think of it as being buried alive. Food was delivered through a slot in the door. Conditions were harsh. There was no air conditioning, no fans. Most cells don't have a window and even if they did, the window would be sealed shut.

For the most part, prisoners were locked down 23 hours a day and any kind of outside contact… visitors, packages, telephone calls… was severely restricted. The only way to relieve the monotony was to read. Dyslexia made reading impossible. I became at expert at twiddling my thumbs.

Like I said earlier, boredom was a big problem in prison. You know that old saying, "Idle hands are the devil's workshop?" Well, in prison, idle hands can become deadly fists very quickly.

There was a time when most prisons were equipped with gyms so that prisoners could take out their frustrations by lifting weights. That turned out not to be such a good idea, especially since the prisoners soon grew bigger and stronger than the guards. The gyms were quickly removed.

That didn't stop us from building our muscles. Prisoners are nothing if not ingenious. One improvised method of weight lifting was to fill laundry bags with sand from the yard. Another was to have one person lift a bottom bed at an angle so that another person could lie down under it. Then, a third person – someone of significant weight – would lay on the bed and the person on the floor would use the bed as a bench press.

By the time I got out of prison, I had powerful upper body strength.

CHAPTER SEVENTEEN

Fear is a useless tactic in prison because most everybody is already afraid. Me? I don't scare easily. The security warden's threats to put me in the box had no effect. If that was what he planned to do, there was no way I could stop him.

"Listen," I tried to explain to him. "I went to the property room. We're allowed to go to the prop room without a pass if we go through medical. That's what I did. Here's the receipt for my stuff."

The warden got nasty. "That's not true. Everybody needs a pass."

I knew it was a losing battle, so I just shrugged my shoulders. "Whatever."

One of them, I'm not sure who, grabbed the receipt from my hand and they both went into the office. Didn't take long before the warden came out and handed me the receipt. I figured he'd made a call and whoever answered told him that I was right. I didn't need a pass.

The guard took me back to my room and, at the first opportunity, I called my dad and told him about the Feds. He already knew. Dad said my name was in the papers. My uncle, who lived in New York, had heard on the news that the Feds were trying to tie me to the mob.

That was the moment I realized something big was going on. The outside world knew more about what was happening to me than I knew. I admit to feeling a little nervous.

The next morning, Duncan came to see me, but he wasn't very encouraging. He was just as much in the dark as I was.

At the time the Feds visited me, I had been in prison about two years and had just filed for my direct appeal. I was afraid they would jeopardize my chance of getting out of jail early. The appeals process is psychological bull shit. It's meant to give a prisoner hope where there isn't any. The courts make a lot of money, but people... people are left bankrupted in more ways than one.

Duncan suggested we play the wait and see game, but I wasn't sure how much more patiently waiting I could handle. The only hope Duncan could give me was his assurance that Bogenschutz was on our side. That seemed like an odd comment. After all, the guy had been my defense attorney. Why wouldn't he be on my side?

It wasn't until weeks later that I found out what a deadly game the Feds were playing. Deadly... for me.

And... I lost my appeal.

On October 18, 2006, Douglas Duncan appeared before the District Court of Appeal of Florida, Fourth District, and argued that the trial court had erred in denying my motion for judgment of acquittal on grounds of self-defense. He also claimed that the court had committed a fundamental error by reading the standard jury instruction on the use of deadly force. Duncan complained that the court confusingly instructed the jury on both a duty to retreat and the absence of a duty to retreat. Because Duncan had not objected to the instructions at trial, the court rejected his argument.

The court also ruled that no error had been found in the Prosecutor's cross-examination of defense witness, Peter Navratil, the young man who worked for me at the deli. It was stated that since I was a sponsor for Peter on his application for an immigration visa, the Prosecutor's questions regarding Peter's immigration status went to bias.

Finally, the court found no fundamental error had occurred in either the prosecutor's cross-examination of me or in closing arguments.

My brother-in-law Tony attended the appeal hearing with David Duncan. David was planning to call him as a witness, but he never got the opportunity to take the stand. According to Tony, the prosecutor kept talking so that Tony wouldn't have a chance to make his statement. When he was finally given a chance to talk, he was interrupted after just five minutes and told that his time was up. He was never able to fully present a plea on my behalf.

After I lost my direct appeal, I was depressed and struggling to stay optimist, but it wasn't easy. I still didn't know why the Feds were interested in me, and not knowing had me imaging all the worst-case scenarios.

Duncan and I talked often but information was scarce. Without much warning, Duncan learned that Federal agents were coming to see me again. Turned out to be the same two guys from the earlier visit.

With Duncan at my side, the interrogation began. The agents spread several photographs of old Italian guys – known mobsters - across the table and asked me if I knew them. One by one, they would touch a photo. "You know this guy?" "How about him?"

My answer was always the same. "I don't know these guys."

We're all familiar with the expression *guilty by association*. All my life, people have associated me with organized crime based solely on my last name and my New York accent. Being Italian pretty much guarantees that people, including the police, will label you "connected."

I don't deny that there were men on the periphery of my life growing up who chose crime as a career path. My dad was a bookie. A few of my uncles were more deeply involved in the syndicate. The reason most men joined the mob was money. They grew up hungry. Literally. Poverty drives good people to commit crimes.

Money was never an issue for me. My dad's bakery was very successful, and I was well paid. Because I could afford to buy whatever I wanted, I had no need to follow in my relatives' footsteps. Could I have gotten involved? Sure. Did I get involved? No. I never forgot… still haven't forgotten… how I felt seeing my dad in the back of that police car when I was a kid. I swore that would never be me.

You know that saying, "Man plans, and God laughs." God must have gotten a real chuckle out of seeing me arrested for killing Gurino. Maybe God, like the police, thinks all Italians are criminals. Or, maybe, preconceived notions are the enemy of the innocent. The first question the prosecutor asked me when I took the stand in my own defense was, "What nationality are you?"

The longer the agents questioned me, the more frustrated they grew. Verbal abuse followed. They began to berate me. "How is it that you don't know these guys?"

See what I mean? The guys in the photos… their last names ended in a vowel. My last name ends in a vowel. That was all the proof the Feds needed. They were convinced we all gathered around a pot of spaghetti on Sunday afternoons for *family* dinner.

I had no clue what they were trying to do, but I was beginning to realize they wanted to entangle me in a case I knew nothing about. The more I said I didn't know the people in the photographs, the angrier the agents became. One guy kept calling me an "asshole." I returned the compliment.

The tall guy got up and stood over me. I'm sitting so he looks even bigger; like a mountain to my ant hill. Intimidation has never worked on me. I may be short of stature, but in my mind I'm eight feet tall.

I looked up at him and said, "You're a real tough guy. Take these cuffs off me and we'll see just how tough you are."

He sneered that he would take the cuffs off if he was able to get me into a federal building. "Then, I'll beat your living ass to a pulp."

I really pissed him off when I responded, "Is it air conditioned? Cause if it is, I'll gladly go."

What did I have to lose? I was already staring at 15 years behind bars. I had no family life. My wife was home with a baby I rarely got to see. She was struggling to make ends meet. What could they do to me that was worse than what I was already going through?

The interrogation had grown quiet; I guess we were all contemplating our next move. It was like a chess game. Suddenly, the Feds ask for me to be removed but ask Duncan to stay. Forty minutes later he tells me that he finally knows what's going on. Never in a million years would I have guessed.

The guy I shot, John Gurino, was no longer a victim. Now, he was a suspect in a high-profile murder case.

The minute Duncan learned the truth, he filed for mitigation of sentence. The mitigation was approved based on the case the Feds were putting together, but the court only reduced my sentence by three years.

The sentence reduction should have been a lot more considering what was now known about Gurino and the fact that the judge in my criminal case – Judge Rapp – wrote a letter stating, "Mr. Liotta is a family man; a business man. He has never been in trouble in the 48 years of his life. The Gurino murder was an isolated incident. He is not a threat to society."

I was very appreciative for Judge Rapp's efforts, but his letter was pretty much ignored. Still three years was something.

Whenever I tell my story, this is where people always ask if I was given clemency. Never… the paperwork didn't even arrive until AFTER I was out of prison.

CHAPTER EIGHTEEN

Okay, so I moved to Florida and went to work for my cousin Dominic. Working with drywall wasn't what I expected. Truthfully, working with my cousin Dominic, Jr., who took over the company after his father died, wasn't what I expected. Me and him... we were nothing alike. Both of us were control freaks and that rarely works out well in business.

My Aunt Jeannie was deep in her grief and wanted nothing to do with the company. Dom was in charge and everyone had to do as he ordered. Since I knew nothing about sheetrock and joint compound, I was given the job of moving materials from one building site to another. The company provided a truck; I provided the muscle.

This was in 1986, well before anyone ever heard of cell phones. We used CB radios to communicate with each other. Dom insisted that I say "Breaker. Breaker." before talking into the microphone. I said, "No way. That's stupid."

What did I know. In North Babylon, we yelled out the car window or whistled when we wanted someone's attention. Whistling was mostly reserved for the good-looking ladies who lived in our neighborhood. Both means of communication were effective. Saying, "Breaker. Breaker," it just seemed stupid.

Dominic tried to pressure me, but I was stubborn. The more Dom insisted, the less I was willing to cooperate. It was a small issue that became a big problem... for Dom, not me. Eventually, we came to an understanding. I would say, "Dom, you there?" into the two-way microphone. Dom would respond, "You have to say 'Breaker Brea...'" I turned off the CB.

When I was in New York, even after I left my dad's bakery, I was making a lot of money. Working for my aunt and cousin was a rude awakening. I got paid $350.00 a week and I worked hard... harder than I had ever worked in my life. There was a lot of physical labor I wasn't used to doing and not a lot of monetary incentive to do it.

I started watching how the business was run. The Mexican construction workers were paid by the number of boards of sheetrock they mounted. They could earn an extra $.50 per sheet if they cleaned the house after the plaster guy was done spackling and sealing the walls.

Sheetrock makes a big mess. There were pieces of unused drywall board all over the place and plaster dust so thick in the air you could choke on it. Every floor had big globs of joint compound stuck to it, which had to be scraped up and thrown away. In multi-story houses, the cleanup could take days but had to be done in hours.

How experienced do you have to be to push a broom and cart trash to a dumpster? My mom had been a tireless housekeeper, so I knew the difference between immaculate and filthy.

I got to thinking that if I did the cleanups, I could make some extra cash. Dominic agreed to give me a try. With my own money, I bought a wheelbarrow, a broom and a shovel. I also bought a Walkman, so I could keep myself company by listening to music.

I formed a plan in my head. Every night, I would start on the top level, dropping large pieces of construction materials to the foyer below. I worked my way down, leaving each floor immaculate as I went. You could eat off of them when I was finished cleaning.

When I got to the first floor, I would load the wheelbarrow with 100-150 pounds of trash and push it to the dumpster. This was never a one trip job.

On every job site, there was a dumpster for trash. It was usually placed a distance from the house, which required pushing the wheelbarrow over the rutted ground, not an easy thing to do. To make it easier, I laid planks from the front of the house to the dumpster, essentially paving a road so that the job would get done faster. It worked great.

By the time I drove away from the job site, every muscle in my body hurt, but I didn't care. I was proud of what I had accomplished and looked forward to having some extra spending money.

Keep in mind that I cleaned the houses at night after working a full day doing my regular job. When payday rolled around, I got two checks.

I had been working for my cousin a few months when the company was hired by a contractor building four houses in the million-dollar range. The contractor had a big dumpster delivered to the site but, because he was building all four houses at the same time, the dumpster filled up fast. When it came time for me to clean, there was no room left in it.

I discussed my concerns with the contractor, who told me not to worry. He suggested I pile whatever I removed from the houses next to the dumpster. He would then get a backhoe to put the trash in the new dumpster he had ordered but which wouldn't be delivered for a few days. That's what I did. Left those four houses sparkling.

It took a few days to finish the cleanup. By the time the last house was done, the new dumpster had arrived. The trash was still on the ground because the contractor hadn't yet gotten the backhoe.

Dom came to the construction site and told me to pick up the trash and put it in the dumpster. I told him the contractor had said to leave it; he would take care of it.

Dom was furious with me and the contractor. I was just plain tired of working my ass off. My days in the house cleaning business had come to an end.

CHAPTER NINETEEN

*A*s I grew more financially independent, I thought it would be best if I moved out of Aunt Jeannie's house. An old friend from New York was living in Fort Lauderdale so I moved in with him. Freedom. I had forgotten what it felt like to be able to come and go as a I pleased.

I still worked days for my cousin, but at night, I became a bouncer in a Fort Lauderdale nightclub making $150 bucks a night, three nights a week. The time clock clicking in my head grew louder.

The confinement I felt living with Aunt Jeannie was nothing compared to being in a jail cell. The ultimate loss of freedom is going to prison. My first day as an official prisoner of the State of Florida was a wake-up call. Life, as I had known it, was over.

First, I was booked and fingerprinted. Then, they took a mug shot. If you think your driver's license photo is bad, trust me, it's nothing compared to the photographic record of an arrest. That picture will haunt you for the rest of your life.

Once all the identification stuff has been completed, they take your personal items, including your clothes and any vestiges of pride you have left.

Privacy is no longer an option. You no longer have a name. You are just a number. I remember thinking that cleaning houses wasn't such a bad gig.

∼

Let me explain to you how a new house is readied for completion. Once most of the construction is done, a punch out list is created. The list contains everything that needs to be fixed to meet the standard expected by the contractor. It was Dom's job to check the sheet-rocked walls.

He would begin by walking from room to room with a pencil and marking x's wherever he saw flaws in the work. I started watching how the punch-out guys made the repairs, and I knew I could do what they were doing. I began by fixing the small stuff, like patching holes around electrical outlets and windows. I was good at it and, in time, got to do entire jobs by myself.

There was this one house… in the $6 million range… that had a long, load-bearing wall on the first floor. When Dominic did his walk through, he saw two places where the wall was bowing outward. He told me to fix it by removing five sheets of wallboard to see where the problem was and what needed to be done.

When Dom left, I cut into the sheetrock in the problem areas. I saw that a 2x4 was only partially set in cement which was causing it to protrude past the allotted space. In other words, the 2x4 stuck out too far for the sheetrock to be flush all the way across the wall.

I used my hammer and chisel to chop away the excess wood and smoothed off the rough edges so that everything was even. Then, I put up new sheetrock, spackled it, and checked for alignment. It was perfect, and I didn't have to waste time and money ripping off five good pieces of wall board.

The next day when I got to work, I found that the area I repaired had been hammered through… big holes everywhere. Dom practically sneered at me, "When I tell you to do something, you do what I say." I'm not an overly sensitive guy, but my feelings were hurt. I handed him my tool belt, wished him good luck, and left. My construction days were over.

 I am grateful for all I learned while working for my cousin. It served me well while I was in prison. Like my father always said, "Un lavoro fatto bene è un lavoro fatto bene la prima volta." Translation: A job well done is a job well done the first time.

CHAPTER TWENTY

How, you are probably asking, did working for my dad and my cousin help me during my 12 years of incarceration. If you think of those jobs only as random stories, they don't have much relevance. But if you look at them as one piece of a much bigger jigsaw puzzle, it will all make sense.

While I was incarcerated at South Bay Correctional Facility in Palm Beach County, I wanted to exercise my custody. Custody refers to the degree of supervision appropriate for an offender. Usually, there are four custody levels:

- Minimum – Inmates who are eligible for outside work assignments.

- Medium – Inmates who are eligible for placement at a work camp.

- Close – Inmates who must remain inside the institutional perimeter and fence.

- Maximum – Inmates on death row.

I wanted to work outside the prison, but because I was in on murder charge, I wasn't allowed while at South Bay.

I've never been good at taking "No" for an answer, so I pleaded my case before the higher ups. I'd already been inside five, maybe, six years and never caused any trouble. However, the prison big shots told me if I kept asking to get outside the gates, they would ship me off to the panhandle because "You're trying to escape." I wasn't. That was the crap they peddled to shut us up.

The next step was to contact Douglas Duncan, my appeals attorney, and beg him to get me on work release. I'm not good at begging either, but if I must, I will. A week and a half later, I heard my name being called out by the inmates who were assigned to the office. "Hey, Liotta, you're leaving tomorrow."

My *what now* question didn't get the answer I expected. I was transferred to Martin County – a level six camp - the worst of the worst. The buildings were old and dirty, rat infested, and there was a lot of dangerous gang activity.

About the rats… the first night at Martin, I was sleeping in the top bunk when I heard a noise. It was pitch black; I couldn't see a thing. From the sound, I thought a cat was trying to get into my locker. I woke up the guy sleeping below me. "You got cats in this place?"

He said, "Ain't no mother fucking cat. It's a rat. We got big ones in here."

Damned if he wasn't right. I had seen a lot of rats coming out of the sewers in New York, but nothing like this one. The only things of interest to a rat in my locker were bags of potato chips. I let him have them.

Back to work release.

~

Although I couldn't exercise my custody at South Bay, going to Martin County made it possible to get the ball rolling. The office assigned me a bunch of different jobs. The first was maintaining the rabbit run.

In a level six camp there is high security. The inmates are separated from the real world by layers of preventative measures. The first deterrent is a high barbed wire fence. Then, there's a section with 12-15 feet of white sand and, finally, another fence with motion and heat sensors. The first fence perimeter is called the Rabbit Run.

Along with five other inmates, I was assigned a hoe, rake, shovel and wheelbarrow. Our job was to remove every weed and tend to the few blades of grass that grew there. It was hot in the sun. The prison leadership intentionally allowed the grounds to go to shit, so the work would be extra hard. Most of the guys hated being there, but I loved it. I was one step closer to the real world.

After proving myself worthy in the rabbit run, I was assigned to clean the Ryce Building, which was where pedophiles used to be housed. It was closed but still needed to be kept clean. Busy work, nothing more. Finally, I was moved to the work camp building, which made it easier for my wife and kids to visit.

Work camp was as close to heaven as I was going to get without dying, and since I had no plans to visit the Pearly Gates any time soon... I was happy for the first time in a long time.

In prison, there is a system for everything. Once in work camp, an inmate is given either a blue card or a white card. With a white card, a prisoner can work anywhere; blue cards only permit a prisoner to work on state grounds. I had a blue card.

My first assignment was to mow the grass at the trailer park where many of the corrections officers lived. That lasted for about five or six months; then I got promoted to white. Having kept my nose clean, I was finally allowed to go off site to work.

Asphalt squad... that's where they put me. For six months, I chipped out old, broken asphalt and loaded it in a truck. Not much different from when I cleaned houses for Dom.

After that I was put on environmental control, cutting down all non-native trees. Wakeup call was 5:30 am. We ate a quick breakfast and headed out; worked until noon when we broke to eat. Lunch was two two-toned bologna sandwiches on white bread. Two toned because the bologna was always half green with mildew. We worked until 6 pm. Next day… same thing.

Occasionally, I was assigned to making barbed wire fences to keep cattle confined. All those odd jobs I had had over the years, I said a silent, "Thank you" every day. I knew my way around a tool box and I was good at physical labor.

CHAPTER TWENTY-ONE

Because I was a good inmate who never caused any problems, my custody allowed me certain privileges. I was assigned to work in the tool room and was put in charge of all the Class A tools. Class As are any tools that can be used as a weapon -- hammers, screwdrivers, saws, utility knives, razor blades. The officer in charge takes the whereabouts of everything in the room very seriously. God forbid something like a utility knife goes missing.

Not everyone could touch the tools. I was working for a female officer who knew she could trust me, so she put me in charge of organizing and logging the inventory. I created a pegboard on which I painted a detailed drawing of each tool. The tools were hung over the drawing when the work day was over.

After my pegboard went up, if anything was missing, it was immediately obvious to the officer in charge. I even painted detailed drawings on the floor for the lawnmowers and larger pieces of equipment.

Since a lot of tools can be used as weapons, it's important to know who checked them out. If a tool is lost, especially a utility knife or a saw, everyone on your crew gets arrested. Everyone gets put into the box until that tool is returned. No exceptions. One person can screw up, but everyone suffers. We could be in the box for 30-60 days while the guards investigated. If the tool wasn't found and no evidence was discovered that it had been intentionally taken, the matter was closed, and the prisoners went back to their normal routine.

Every day prisoners are driven to their work assignment – the work camp, trailer park or main unit. The trailer park was right next to the tool room, maybe 500-600 feet away, but prisoners were still driven from one place to another. One morning, I was in the tool room when the officer in charge notifies me that officers from the main unit are coming to get me. I asked why but he was just as much in the dark as I was. I kept thinking the worst... my father had died, one of my kids had gotten seriously ill. I was worried, but what could I do. I sat and waited for them to arrive.

When the officers got there, they told me I wasn't in any trouble but even so, they needed to handcuff me. I was brought back to the work camp and strip searched. I never caused any trouble, but I was still treated like the lowest of the low.

Once I was cleared, the handcuffs were removed, and the officers walked me to the main building. As I was being led to my case worker's office, all the officers assigned to this building were looking at me with a weird expression on their faces. It was unnerving.

My case worker was talking to some guy I didn't know, but I immediately recognized him as a Fed. They have a distinctive look about them best described as arrogance dressed in a cheap suit.

I was worried because I was going on work release and I didn't want anything to screw that up. The FBI guy said not to worry. He just wanted to know what I planned to do when I was released from prison. Jokingly, I said, "I don't know. Maybe, I'll just retire."

He immediately asked, "How are you going to do that? You got extra money laying around somewhere?" My nerve endings started to tingle. I asked if I needed a lawyer and the FBI guy responded, "Do you want a lawyer?"

I tried to lessen the tension by saying, "You know what? I'm going to go outside and come back in. I'll pretend this conversation didn't just happen."

I still had no idea why they were there or what they wanted from me. I just knew that something was up, and it could ruin my chances of going home. The agent made no further attempt to talk to me. He wished me luck and left.

CHAPTER TWENTY-TWO

During one of my stints doing environmental cleanup, I was assigned to a team supervised by a corrections officer by the name of Brimmery. COs did not carry guns, but they did have a can of mace and a panic button on their belts. Mostly, they relied on their relationship with the prisoners in their charge to maintain order. Brim had five inmates under his supervision. He was a big man and didn't need any help keeping us under control. Trust me on that.

Of all the corrections officers, Brim was my favorite. He often joked with us while out in the field. It was standard operating procedure for him to assign each of us a specific duty. Some guys were assigned to cutting down trees, usually with a chain saw or a machete. The tree cutters had to go deep into the woods, clearing a path as they went.

I had responsibility for spraying the newly cut areas so that the plants and trees didn't grow back. I hated that job for two reasons. The mosquitoes were literally man-eaters, and it required wearing a heavy sprayer filled with weed killer on my back to which a long tube and a nozzle were attached.

Sometimes two sprayers worked side by side, especially when we needed to cover a densely overgrown area. In the summer, sweat dripped from our every pore in less than 30 minutes. Hours were spent out in the heat and humidity with barely a break for water.

Mostly, the same guys work together. We all knew each other because we lived together in the work camp dormitory. One day, I was working with a guy named Koy. He was a tough kid, urban ghetto type, maybe 20-25 years old, whose face, neck and body were covered with tattoos.

Koy was a ball buster, always starting fights for no reason. To live well in prison, you must have a steady supply of cash, so you can buy what you need. Koy didn't have any money. He tried to bully people into giving him whatever he wanted.

Okay. So, Koy and I were working together. I had the sprayer. He had the machete. I'm not a tree hugger; I'm much happier in the concrete jungle. Mother Nature is not high on my list of persons to be admired. Koy thought differently.

Rather than cutting the trees at the beginning of a path, he made his way deep into the overgrowth. I asked him to stop. Just the thought of a face to face with a snake made my skin crawl.

My first day on environmental duty remains vivid in my mind. An old timer told me to watch out for snakes. I took his words to heart and kept staring at the ground. Seeing how intent I was at watching where I was going, he started laughing.

"You better look up. They're in the trees, too."

I nearly had a heart attack. I didn't know snakes could climb trees. In New York, snakes have two legs and walk right up to you on the sidewalk.

Anyway, Koy and I started arguing; he insisted that I follow him off the trail and deep into the woods. There was no way I was going to do that, so I quickly emptied my sprayer and returned to the van where Brim was waiting.

Like a man with a mission, Koy followed me. I refilled my sprayer and waited. Brim told me to get my ass back out in the field. I refused.

There was no way I was going back into the woods with Koy. As nice a guy as Brim was, he could also get nasty when an inmate challenged him. Leaving no room for discussion, he ordered me to go with Koy.

I lost my cool and started yelling and kicking things. I could see Brim's hand reaching for the panic button. I thought for sure he was going to call for backup, but he knew I wasn't a trouble maker, so he stopped and let the matter rest.

On our way back to work camp, Koy sat in the back of the van and began threatening me. He claimed he was going to "get me" when we get back to our dorm.

I told him, "You don't have to wait. Bring it on."

Brim yelled for us to calm down, but Koy continued to curse at me the whole trip.

To be honest, I was worried that if Brim told anyone what had happened, I could be arrested. Yeah, you can get arrested while you are in prison. It's just how the system works; a way of keeping the prisoners under control. I was due to be released in a few weeks, and I didn't want anything to screw that up.

When we got back to camp, Koy ran through the strip shack – that's where we were cleared to return to our dorm – and disappeared before I could say or do anything. I was prepared for an ambush, looking over my shoulder, waiting for him to come at me. I got to our room and there he was sound asleep in his bed.

I nudged him. "Koy, what's up. I thought you wanted to fight me."

He said, "Go away, old man. I don't want to hurt you."

"You don't want to hurt me? You almost got me arrested with that act of yours."

As if on cue, Brim came in and pulled me aside. Other guards had heard what had happened out in the field. They told me that Brim was doing me a big favor by not reporting me. On their advice, I cooled off and let the matter drop. In prison, everybody is always trying to prove something. None of it ever makes any sense.

Oddly enough, after that day, Koy became my best friend... or, at least, he thought he was my best friend.

Quick story... the side of the work van was stenciled in letters big enough that a blind man could see *Environmental Cleanup*. It was clearly stated that we were on prison release and performing a service for the county.

This one day, the police and a news crew showed up. The police had their guns drawn. There wasn't one inmate there who hadn't seen his share of violence, but cops with guns was a good reason to be afraid. The reason for their unexpected arrival was that the neighbors had called and reported that men with machetes were terrorizing the residents.

We almost got shot because a few people decided to overreact to something that was clearly not a danger. I felt my anger meter rising. Here I had come close to dying at the hands of a crazy man who forced me to defend myself in a do or die manner, and now I was facing death again because people hadn't bothered to read a warning sign. What an obituary that would have made.

My gut tells me the media would never have printed the facts in their entirety. Fiction sells more papers than the truth.

CHAPTER TWENTY-THREE

Even though Dom and I had parted ways, we didn't stop being family... blood being thicker and all that stuff. We both had tempers that were quick to ignite and equally quick to fizzle out. No harm. No foul. Before long, we were back to working together, just not in the drywall business, which had gone under shortly after I quit.

Before I even came to Florida, my dad had been sending his flatbread crackers to the family to sell, but they didn't know how to do the marketing. Selling was in my blood. I was itching to get back to what I knew best -- convincing restaurant owners that they should serve dad's crackers to their customers. I knew that if I could sign up enough places to buy the crackers, I'd have a steady income, one that would grow quickly.

After I moved to Florida, Dad's bakery took a turn for the worst. He was trying to do everything himself, but that just wasn't possible. No longer was he baking the crackers; now he was buying them from a supplier - a decision which added to the cost of his operation. He repackaged the purchased crackers under the Sunshine Flats label and continued selling them to his customers, but it was getting harder and harder to make payroll every week.

At my suggestion, we revamped the company. Dad sent the crackers to me and, using a $20,000 investment from Aunt Jeanne, I ordered specially designed boxes and labels and started Rosario's Flatbread Crackers. Aunt Jeanne's son, Glenn, was also an investor, but he quickly wanted out. He had little to no interest in the cracker business.

Dominic, now out of the sheetrock business, and his wife Valerie handled the office side of our company. Aunt Jeanne's garage became our warehouse. Every month, a tracker trailer would deliver stock to the house. There were 150 cases to a skid, and each delivery carried two to three skids.

Once everything was ready, I bought a van and began making sales the old-fashioned way – door to door. I would go to one restaurant and tell them that their competitor was buying our crackers. Once I had that account secured, I'd go to the competitor and tell them that the other restaurant was buying the crackers. Every week, I traveled from Key Biscayne to Melbourne, doing different sections of the route each day. Pretty soon, I was selling three to four skids a week.

One of my favorite sales tricks was to enter a restaurant through the back door… like I was staff. Wearing plastic gloves, I would open a box of crackers and put them in bread baskets. Then, I would go into the main dining room and offer a sample to patrons. Everybody loved the crackers!

Some of the managers got angry that I had invaded their territory, but once they saw their customers' reactions, they were sold. I would leave a free case and, within a day or two, the manager would call and place an order.

The business was growing fast, which to me was a sign that we should expand. I decided to give individual packaging a try. Remember, I was only selling in bulk up to this point, but bulk doesn't work for convenience stores, delicatessens, farm stands and small retail markets. For these businesses, we sold 12 packages to a box with one package retailing for $1.79. Another success!

∼

Another time, I stopped at a farm stand in Miami. It was a canvas tent operation with lots of produce available for sale. The parking lot was packed with cars; a good indicator that business was booming.

The farm stand was run by a Venezuelan family. At first, they said the crackers weren't any good... not healthy enough even though they only had two grams of fat. I told the owner's wife about *The Boys* and she agreed to put two cases at each of the two registers. To sweeten the deal, I put an open bulk package between the registers for customers to taste. Then, I left.

I was walking through the parking lot when I saw a Hispanic woman with four kids in tow. Cautiously, I approached her and told her about the crackers. I said I would give her a bulk case for free plus $5.00 to each kid if she would do me a favor.

I asked if they would go into the store and each buy two packages of crackers, using my money. She thought I was crazy, but she did it. I left not knowing if my idea would work.

A short time later, Valerie called me from the office and told me to go back to the farm stand. They wanted to place an order.

I called the owner's wife and told her I couldn't get there until the following week as I was too far away. That was a lie. I was within a half hour's drive, but I didn't want to appear too anxious to get her business. She asked me how many flavors the crackers came in. I told her six and, if she ordered ten cases, I'd give her one case for free. She said, "If you come back today, I'll take 30 cases." I turned the van around.

On my way back to the farm stand, I stopped at a Publix and bought a few potato chip racks for $20.00 from the truckers on the loading dock. I used the racks to display the crackers at the farmstand. The wife and her husband became good, long time customers.

Dom and Valerie continued handling the administrative end of the business. Not being formally educated, I was unable to deal with the extensive paperwork and daily bookkeeping, especially when it came to the corporate accounts. I was happy to let Dom and Val shoulder that responsibility.

CHAPTER TWENTY-FOUR

I'm a big believer in fate. Everything happens for a reason but, sometimes, you don't find out what that reason is until much later. That's how it was with me and many of my long time friends.

Anyone living in south Florida has shopped at a farmer's market. In years past, these markets were nothing more than a canopied open-air stand set up at the side of a road. With little protection from the weather and the need to deal with temperatures hot enough to fry eggplant, it took dedication to keep these markets going. A few people... those who had a strong work ethic and a nose for business, were eventually able to expand into full-service grocery stores.

Because my bread was popular with customers who shopped at these markets, I got to know many of the families. One owner in particular, Gio, was very old fashioned and strict. The first time we came face to face - back in my flatbread cracker days - I was sporting a ponytail and earrings. He took one look at me, pronounced my crackers "... no good," and told me he didn't need them. I think he expected me to knuckle under and adopt a fashion style he thought suitable, but as you know by now, I've never been the type to take orders. Much to Gio's surprise, when he told me the crackers were "... no good," I became even more determined to sell them to him.

Utilizing my gift for gab, I went into negotiation mode and offered him a case of crackers as well as some individual packages for free. He accepted. A few days later, I went back to the stand. Gio said, "I'll buy your crackers, but you've got to get rid of the hair and the earrings." I refused.

He couldn't believe I would pass up his business. We were standing in the hot parking lot, sweat pouring off our foreheads, when he said, "You're willing to lose this gold mine for a ponytail and earrings? You're crazy."

I smiled just like I did each time my friend Michael would bet against who I knew and who I didn't know. Gio said, "Okay. Bring me the crackers. I'll take 40... no, 50 cases a week." That was the start of a lifelong friendship.

Let me tell you why I respect this man so much.

Gio, despite his dislike of my fashion sense, was one of the few people who believed in me. He saw that I was more than just a capable baker with a product that people craved. He recognized that together we could both grow our businesses by giving people what they wanted.

At his suggestion, I opened a small bakery inside his market. This was similar to the way my dad had had a carpenter build shelves at farmer's markets back in Long Island to sell his bread.

Setting up a bakery at an open-air market is not as easy as it might seem. There was no way I could install ovens on premises, so I had to find a suitable location off site where I could do the actual baking. Then, there was the matter of delivering the fresh breads and pastries to the market every day. I do love a challenge, so I was as excited about finding a solution as I was about opening a store.

The bakery was a success from day one. Truthfully, as word spread, it was rare if a line wasn't forming by the time we opened each morning. Gio became like a second father to me. He holds a special place in my heart.

Now, as supportive as Gio was to me, he was also a perfectionist who demanded his employees aspire to the same standards as he did.

Some mornings, I would help his workers arrange the produce that would be on sale that day.

Gio had a vision of how he expected his tables to look. It could take as long as five hours to separate the fruits and vegetables and arrange them properly. Some days, we redid the displays three or four times before he gave us his seal of approval. The work was backbreaking, but no one dared say a word. Gio was… still is… a tough old guy, but he never expected anyone to do something he wouldn't do himself.

Mama Gio was also a hard worker. She did all the bookkeeping, putting in long hours to make the business a success. Together, she and her husband were unstoppable. They were two of the most dedicated people I have ever met.

During a lull in business one morning, I asked Gio how he had gotten into the produce business. I swear I've never known anyone else with such an extensive knowledge of the gifts from the garden. He told me that when he was a little boy, he would work beside his father as he sold fresh produce from the back of a truck. They worked New York's inner-city neighborhoods; the same neighborhoods his grandfather and great grandfather had worked before him.

Eventually, Gio and his wife decided to move to Florida. Their children were grown, and the winters were hard on them. Instead of retiring, they bought a pickup truck and sold tomatoes by the side of the road. In time, their children also moved south and worked beside their parents.

Who would have thought that a punk-ass baker sporting a ponytail and earrings would find a supporter in an old-world Italian and that a life-long friendship would born out of a mutual love for flour, water and yeast.

CHAPTER TWENTY-FIVE

While numbers on a balance sheet don't lie, the true indicator that your product is selling well is when you receive phone calls from your competitors. I had been pounding the beat signing up new customers for about 12 months when we got a call from Sysco, probably the biggest food service provider in the world. Valerie took the call in the office and passed the message on to me, "Joe Piazza wants to talk to you."

Joe was responsible for Sysco's Italian products line. He asked if I would come to Sysco's southeast office to talk because my flatbread crackers were cutting into the sales of their crackle bread, a popular item in restaurants all over Florida. I told Joe that my crackers weren't Italian despite my name being on the label. They were more in line with Jewish matzo bread. He still wanted a meeting.

We set a date for the following week. I was nervous. Sysco was the big time. We're talking executive board room, expensive suits and $500-a-pair shoes. I didn't even own a sports jacket, and my Sunday go-to-meeting footwear was a pair of well-worn Nikes.

Aunt Jeanne gave me one of my late Uncle Dom's suits, and I had it altered. Clothes may make the man, but I wasn't fooling anyone. I'm not a suit and tie guy. I'm most comfortable in jeans and a tee shirt. Trying to be someone I wasn't made me feel foolish.

Dom and I went to the meeting together. It's always good to have back up in new situations. One of the first questions Joe asked me was how many trucks we had. I said, "A couple." We only had one, but I figured what the hell. If he's asking questions, I've got an advantage.

Joe took Dom and me into the board room, where we laid out samples of our flatbreads and a variety of spreads in plastic shell-shaped dishes. Four corporate types joined us. They ate the crackers and seemed to like them.

Then, another guy came into the room. He was about 60 and big... not tall... big and a bit disheveled looking. His shirt was half out of his pants and his tie was askew. The four guys at the table jumped up as though God had suddenly appeared. I took one look at him and, immediately, I felt very fashionable in my dead uncle's suit.

The big man began to ask me questions like how did I manage to sign up so many accounts? I told him, "I'm a back-door man. I never enter a potential account through the main entry like ordinary salesmen. I don't dress like a salesman either.

My uniform is a pair of work boots and a clean tee shirt because I want the kitchen help to see me as one of their own. I say, 'Hello' and begin to talk to everyone... the chef, the sous chef, the kitchen porter... even the dishwasher. I give them all samples of my crackers.

Sooner or later, the restaurant manager or owner will wander in. He doesn't know what to make of me, but I'm personable and so he listens to my spiel. Finally, I say, "I know you're busy. Let me give you some free samples. I promise you, your customers will love them.'

Then, I leave. The product sells itself."

While I was explaining my sales pitch, the big man was eating like there was no tomorrow. Cracker crumbs and butter were stuck to his mouth and cheeks. His obvious enjoyment gave me confidence, but when I finished talking, he remained silent. I started to tell him some funny stories and he laughed in all the right places.

Eventually, he pushed himself away from the table. "You're very entertaining. I gotta go. Good meeting you." And he was gone. I didn't know what to make of the situation.

The minute the big man was out of sight, the other four executives relaxed. They told me that Joe was the president of Sysco. I was stunned. Here was this powerful guy listening to my stories which, to be honest, I told in some rough language. I figured I was doomed.

The first four guys left, and three new guys came in. They said that the big man wanted my product, and it was their job to do whatever was necessary to make that happen. Me and Dom, we looked at each other and tried not to smile.

Joe Piazza began to coordinate the deal. My price was high; Joe said that if I lowered it, they would buy in large quantities. We came to a meeting of the minds.

In time, with the product selling even more briskly than expected, Sysco decided it would be in their favor to rebrand the crackers under their private label, Sysco Supreme. They wanted control of all the customers we shared. I was okay with that, but I also had private customers of my own who did not buy through Sysco. I wasn't willing to give those up.

It took a little negotiating, but my terms were met. Sysco got all the corporate accounts and I kept my private customers. The only stipulation was that I not give those customers to a Sysco competitor. I agreed because what Sysco didn't know was that I was making more money from the private accounts than I was with them.

Everybody was happy. Dom and Valerie continued handling our business affairs. Even today, many years after that deal was struck, Dom is still doing business with Sysco and Rosario's Flatbread Crackers are still popular.

CHAPTER TWENTY-SIX

Here's where fate comes into my story.

I was out on bail in the Gurino case and I needed work. The cracker business was no more. Another hard lesson learned which I'll explain later. For now, I needed money. Getting out of jail isn't free.

I started making produce deliveries for Gio, whose business savvy had made him a successful grocer. We had become good friends during the years he was buying my flatbread crackers. A popular Delray steakhouse was on my route. In the restaurant's store room were cases of their in-house garden vegetable salad dressing... a popular item which they bottled and sold to their customers.

Gio suggested we buy the salad dressing business from the steakhouse owner. Seemed like a good idea so I said, "Sure." We offered him $100,000.00. He wanted a million. There was no way we were going to pay that kind of money for oil and vinegar.

The idea was a good one, and I wasn't about to give up so easily. I bought a few bottles of the dressing thinking, "How hard could this be to make? Maybe, we could make our own."

Of course, Gio thought I was crazy. He didn't believe we could duplicate the original; he felt we'd be wasting time and money trying.

Another challenge. I studied the contents label on the original dressing bottle. Nothing unusual jumped out at me... garlic, ginger, vinegar, sugar, oil and soy sauce. Normal stuff. I already knew that the ingredients were listed by highest quantity to lowest quantity.

The next day I went to a local market and bought everything I needed. The dressing I made was close in taste to the original, but it wasn't perfect.

An idea hit me. I dumped the contents onto a baking tray and put the tray in the freezer. Know why I did that? Not to get too technical, but the molecules in each ingredient determine how long it will take that ingredient to freeze. By pulling the tray out of the freezer every 15 minutes and stirring the dressing, I was able to separate all the parts. Each was put into a separate cup, melted and weighed.

By now, my mom and dad had moved to Florida. It was great having them nearby, and my dad was my go-to guy whenever I had an idea. He was gung-ho about the salad dressing and wanted to help make it.

We mixed up another batch; this time making a gallon, but it still wasn't right. The original dressing was darker in color and had a slightly nutty flavor. I went to the nearby Asian market and asked the clerk some questions. He told me to buy sesame oil. He also told me that soy sauce came in different varieties. The one I needed was *dark*.

We threw the first batch away and started again. Winner! Winner! Chicken dinner!

No one believed I had created the exact same product, so to taste test it, I washed a no-longer-full bottle of the original dressing and refilled it with my dressing. Then, I filled plates with iceberg lettuce and poured a little of my dressing and a little of the original on top. "Go ahead. Eat it. Which is which?" I was daring them to tell the difference.

Interesting how you can know people for years and still they can think you're a liar. To a man, everybody thought I had put the original on both salads. Even when I showed them the five-gallon container my dad and I had made, they didn't believe me. It took a lot of convincing, but Bobby Chang's Salad Dressing was born that night. We made a sugar-free variety and a cranberry version to go along with the original.

Gio was happy with the results of my experiment, but he said the true taste test would be with customers. I set up a table at the market and offered little paper cups filled with lettuce and some of the dressing but, while I displayed bottles of the original dressing, I poured our dressing on the salad. I never told the customers what I was doing.

At the end of the day, we had sold 30 cases of the original. The only complaint was that some people felt it was too sweet for diabetics. That's how the sugar-free variety of our dressing came to be.

In short order, I found a company that would bottle the dressing if there were no peanuts in it… allergies and all. The owner walked me through the process, explained how certain items can be toxic, and tested our dressing to make sure all the ingredients were safe. We were in business.

Getting the dressing to market was a lot of work. While the bottling company would *make* the dressing, I had to arrange with vendors to deliver all the ingredients to the warehouse. I also had to provide the labels. The dressing was made 130 gallons at a time, which filled 100 cases. There were 12 bottles in each case.

Sales were going great until I went to prison. No matter what business you are in, working with vendors is a hassle. Without me to do the leg work, the business died. The steakhouse went out of business around the same time.

Okay. So that's the salad story. You can see that I'm an out of the box thinker. I see solutions where other people see problems. Unfortunately, when a problem arose that threatened everything I had worked to build, I didn't see it until it was too late.

CHAPTER TWENTY-SEVEN

A good way to get exposure for food products is to have a display at restaurant trade shows. These conventions provide major networking opportunities because they are attended by world leaders looking for new ideas in food and beverage products. Dom, Valerie, Aunt Jeanne and I did as many of them as possible – sometimes 10 a year.

Dom and Val did a good job making our sales pitch to buyers, but it was me they really came to see. I was the P.T. Barnum of these events... I never met a person I didn't like (at least, they thought I liked them) and who didn't like me. I have the *gift of gab*, which is every salesman's unique gift. Without it, I would still be hanging sheetrock.

While on the surface, our little family business seemed to be humming smoothly, there were problems brewing under the surface.

I was named for my grandfather, Rosario "Ralph" Liotta. Like so many Italians who wanted to fit into their new home in America, grandpa anglicized his name by changing it to Ralph. He took it as his middle name but used it as his first name.

During my youth I also used Ralph as my given name. During the Gurino trial, news reporters took it upon themselves to label me Ralph, which really annoyed me. If you look up Rosario Liotta on the internet, you won't find any news articles. Look up Ralph Liotta, man, there's a ton of articles, mostly filled with lies.

Anyway, troubles began to surface during a convention in Marco Island. When I picked up my vendor I.D. badge, it was made out in the name of Ralph Liotta. I knew I hadn't filled out the paperwork that way, and Dom and Val denied doing it. Something was fishy.

I had the badge corrected which, for some reason, infuriated my aunt and cousins. It seemed weird to me, but I was busy selling and put the matter out of my head. It wasn't until a potential customer asked how we had come up with the name for our crackers – Rosario's Flatbread Crackers – that I realized how big a problem I had.

Aunt Jeannie told the buyer that the crackers were named for her father. I overheard her talking and said, "We didn't name the crackers after grandpa. He knew nothing about crackers. The product is named for me because I started the company." You could have heard the explosion on the other side of the world.

Aunt Jeanne, Dom and Val called a company meeting. They told me I had to give them more shares. In return, Dom would take care of all the corporate accounts. I agreed, but I wasn't happy about it.

Shortly after the attempted coup, Dom and I made a delivery to Sysco. Sysco's offices were in the same complex as Publix corporate offices. Access was through a guard gate and only by appointment.

I pulled the van up to the booth and said to the guard, "I've got a great cracker here I'd like to show to whoever is in charge. Six flavors – you'll love them all." The guard told me I needed a pass; he couldn't let me in without authorization.

I said "Thanks" and handed him six cases of crackers. The gate went up. Inside the corporate offices, I left 12 cases – two of each flavor – with the receptionist along with a stack of business cards and literature. I was honest with her. Said I didn't have an appointment but, if she could see to it that the buyer in charge got a few of the samples, I would be grateful. She smiled. I smiled. Dom and I left.

Four days later, Val told me that some guy from Publix was trying to get a hold of me. I called him, and the first thing he said was, "I'm sitting in my office eating your crackers. How, the hell, did you get them in here?"

I told him, "It's top secret. I can't tell you." He laughed; said he loved them but was concerned because if I could get through their security, then anybody could get through. I still wouldn't reveal how I did it.

We set up a meeting. The buyer said, "I love your product and I'm willing to give you 25 stores to start, but I need to know how you got the crackers in here." Luckily, he really liked the flatbreads because I refused to tell him.

Most people don't know that there is a process to getting a product into a large supermarket like Publix. The guy in the corporate office sent me to a distributor who would sell the product. Remember, John Englishman, the food broker who helped my dad? Well, a distributor does the same thing.

Typically, when a product is chosen to be sold in a store, the manufacturer pays a slot fee. This is rent for the shelf space the product will utilize. Since we had six flavors, we needed a lot of shelf. I asked the distributor what it was going to cost us. He said, "Buddy, you don't have to pay nothing. Publix wants your product, so the space is free."

After so many years, our flatbread crackers... my father's flatbread crackers... were finally in Publix. We had come full circle. I made sure that every store was happy. We delivered a quality product and set up beautiful displays. That was in 1988. Publix still carries our brand.

CHAPTER TWENTY-EIGHT

Right about this time, I got a call from Joe, the president of Sysco. He asked me to meet him for lunch in North Miami. When we were through eating, he got around to why he wanted the meet.

"Rosario," he said, "you're an unbelievable seller. I want you to teach my guys how to sell our products. We have 40 salesmen; I want you to ride along with all of them."

We did what I called cracker stops. It took a few months, but when everyone was trained, sales went up and Joe was happy.

Dom wanted to show our appreciation to the Sysco executives for their continued business, so he invited them to a holiday dinner party in Fort Lauderdale. There were 12 people plus me, my date, Dom and Valerie. I was sitting at the head of the table; my date was to my left and Dom was to my right. The first course was soup.

I was in the middle of eating when Dom asked me to meet him in the bathroom for a private talk. He told me that I was embarrassing him by making too much noise while I ate my soup. He said I was "… slurping" and emphasized that these were *classy* people. I needed to learn the rules of etiquette.

Do you remember the story about the first time I met the president of Sysco at their offices... crackers and butter stuck to his face? Yeah. I remember that day, too.

I nodded at Dom and returned to the table. I was so angry; I didn't bother to sit down. I merely picked up my soup bowl, turned it over and walked out. Later, I heard from the guests that they thought it was hilarious.

∼

Manners aren't a big priority when you're in prison. As I said earlier, there is a system for everything - even eating. At South Bay, inmates had to order their food on a bubble sheet. These are order forms that are turned in on a weekly basis. After they are turned in, a warehouse processes them and delivers the food.

At mealtimes, the inmates are taken to the canteen where they pick up their food. The meals are charged against their accounts.

Yeah. You pay for your food in some prisons. At least, you do if you want to eat anything decent.

The day I arrived at South Bay, two tough guys decided to see what I was made of... meaning whether they could intimidate me. If they could, I'd be their whore for however long I was at that prison.

As I was filling out my bubble sheet, they came up behind me and demanded, "Hey, man, get us some coffee." I knew what they were doing, but I played along. "Okay. I'll get you both coffee." Of course, I didn't.

Five days later, I went to the canteen to eat. I was hungry and looking forward to eating the meatball hero I had ordered. As I was waiting for my dinner, one of those tough guys came up to me and asked, "Hey, man, did you get the coffee?"

I answered, "They ran out."

He started to rant, "They didn't fucking run out."

I knew this was a test. If I got up and brought him coffee, he would make me do it every day. It would be a sign of weakness. So, I threw my sandwich against the wall and yelled, "Listen, mother fucker, you want coffee? I don't have any coffee. Here's my fucking sandwich. You can eat it. I don't know who the fuck you are, and I don't care. You wanna fight? You can fight me for the coffee."

I was screaming like an animal. It was an act, and it worked. The guy backed away. "Hey, dude, take it easy."

I said, "Go fuck yourself."

When I turned around, I saw the meatballs sliding down the wall. I was starving… wanted to eat that sandwich so badly. I didn't, but somebody did.

Nobody ever asked me for coffee again.

∼

While the beginning of the end had been coming for a long time between Dom and me, the soup incident was the straw that broke the family business apart.

A few weeks later I got bronchitis. I was sick and could not go to work. Dom insisted that I get out of bed and get my ass to the office. See, if I didn't go to work, Dom would have to make the deliveries, and he didn't want to do that. He was or, at least, he thought he was an executive. He only handled the corporate end of the business.

No amount of threats was going to make me get better any quicker. I can't remember ever before or since being that sick. I was out for a week and no deliveries were made. The customers were angry, but Dom felt driving a truck was below him.

My first day back, I got a call from Dom telling me he was at a lawyer's office, and he was staging a takeover. He said that my attitude made me a hostile partner. I was beyond caring. We split the corporation. Dom took the corporate accounts and I took the retail ones.

I rented a warehouse and hired two drivers to cover my routes. They started stealing from me almost immediately. That was enough for me. I called Dom and gave him the retail accounts. He turned around and gave them away.

Dom still owns the corporate part of the business. He still has our accounts with Publix and Sysco. He and Val... they're divorced.

I truly believe that when one door closes, another one opens. Sometimes, you might have to give it a shove.

CHAPTER TWENTY-NINE

Walking away from the cracker business was hard. I had put my heart and soul into it, and I felt betrayed by my family. Plus, I missed the challenge of signing up new customers and the interaction with people I met along the routes. Since I'm not good at doing nothing, I took a full-time job at my friend Nick's Italian fish restaurant.

Even while the cracker business was going strong, I helped Nick out at night and on weekends. Working at his restaurant was like coming home. It felt right. I brought my Dad in to make fresh bread on the premises. Customers loved it! In fact, they loved Dad's bread so much that I decided to start a new wholesale bakery. You might say, I was going back to my roots.

It's rare for me to lose a friend or acquaintance even if a lot of time passes without seeing them. I knew a lot of delivery guys from working the cracker routes for so many years. We stayed friends even after Dom and I parted ways.

A few phone calls and the drivers began picking up the rolls at the warehouse and delivering samples to restaurants, delicatessens and supermarkets. Before long, those businesses canceled contracts with their existing vendors and signed on with us. The companies that lost the accounts also signed on with us. They had no choice… it was our bread, or they were going to run out of dough in more ways than one.

When I started the bakery, I began with one bay in a low rent area of Deerfield Beach and one van. We began by making hero rolls, which were of the highest quality. The business took off immediately. I soon needed another bay and additional trucks. To keep up with the demand for our products, I brought my brother Anthony from New York. Anthony was the actual baker while I was the front man.

Two bays became four bays. Each one was about 2,000 square feet. I hired two guys and taught them how to bake. During the day, my brother and I did the baking. Starting around 5 pm, the new guys would come in and keep the ovens going through the night. I came back at 2 am to pick up my deliveries; I would be out on the road for hours.

The bays had over-sized garage type doors. Since this was Florida, it was summertime almost all year long. There was no a/c, and the heat from the ovens was intense. We had to leave the doors up to get ventilation. I did install a fan, but it just didn't provide enough relief.

One morning when I arrived at the bakery, I knew something had happened. Both of my workers were upset, and one of them was crying. They told me that a couple of guys from the hood – gang members - had robbed them.

My guys had been told from the start that if anyone came in who was hungry, "… give them bread. Make a friend of them." The gang members weren't looking for friendship. They took my guys wallets. One of my men had a chain that his mom had given him. It was special to him. He was more upset about that than he was about losing money. They gang members didn't hurt my guys, but they did scare them.

To guarantee there would be no more problems, I hired a chain link fence company to put up poles and two gates which would lock in the center. The gates were on the outside of the garage doors. This way, my men could open the garage doors from the inside, but no one could get in through the gate unless they had a key. They were safe and no longer felt afraid.

A few mornings later as I was loading my truck, two strange guys showed up. The gate was open because I was there. These guys came walking in all sure of themselves. They asked if I had any bread I could give them.

Trust me, there was always extra bread, so I took a few loaves off the cooling rack and put them in bags. While I was doing this, I noticed that my bakers looked uneasy. When the two strangers left, my guys told me that one of them had stolen the chain. I ran outside and yelled, "Hey, wait a minute. Come over here. I want to talk to you." The guy who took the chain answered, "Talk about what?" I said, "I want to talk to you. Come on over here."

Both began to lip off, "We ain't got no time for conversation with you." I started walking toward them, and the next thing I knew, there was a gun pointed at me. "Don't come any closer."

I stopped walking. "Okay, I won't come any closer, but let me tell you something. If you come back inside my bakery, you'll see what happens to tough guys who steal from my workers. Don't let me see you back here in this neighborhood."

They walked away, but if I hadn't confronted them, they might have kept coming back.

My business was growing quickly, and the ovens I had did not meet the demand. To make enough bread for my customers, I bought two traveler ovens from a guy in St. Armand's, Florida. The ovens came from Kentucky Fried Chicken. At one time, KFC baked all the rolls they served in their restaurants. They would freeze them and ship them all over the country.

These ovens were huge. They each held 118 sheet pans. When joined together, they measured 30 feet x 15 feet and reached 2 million BTUs. While the ovens were being assembled, they looked like a Sherman Tank. There were two pieces on one side and three pieces on the other side, plus a front and a back. Once the outer panels were installed, it looked like what it was -- a gigantic oven.

Whatever bread was left over after my drivers had picked up their orders was packed in bags and put on a rack at the front of the bakery. Every day, the people in the neighborhood came and took whatever they wanted. I knew there were families who didn't have a lot of money to buy food, so I was happy to give the bread away. It was the right thing to do.

In the beginning, people would throw the bread trays all over the parking lot. I put up a sign and asked that they stack the trays neatly on the rack. They did. The residents were grateful, and we never had another problem.

There was one very feeble man… he looked like he was 90 years old. He would take bread and make bread pudding. A few days a week, he brought enough for my guys to eat with their lunch. One day, I stopped him to thank him. I asked his name and realized that he was a she. A lady was making the bread pudding. She was always dressed like a man, so I never guessed.

CHAPTER THIRTY

My bread was of the best quality, but quality isn't worth anything if you can't get your products to the consumer. I had an idea.

When I first started the bakery, I did the baking and some of the deliveries. I had two vans. One I used to cover my routes, and the other was driven by a man I hired to make deliveries. As the business grew, I bought more trucks and hired more drivers. They were paid $500 a week.

The problem with that was the overhead. Between the payments on the trucks, the gas and repairs, the insurance, the drivers' salaries, I was putting out a lot of money. I talked to the drivers and explained how they could become independent contractors and, essentially, be their own boss.

Some of the drivers already owned trucks. Others, I gave the opportunity to buy my trucks – the ones they had been driving all along. Each of the drivers was given a chance to buy the route they had been selling to for however long they had worked for me.

Most people don't realize that the trucks they see in a supermarket parking lot delivering groceries are not necessarily owned by the company making the product being delivered. If the truck has a company logo on it, it is probably corporate, but if the logo is that of a hauling company, then the driver is an independent contractor (I.C.) hired to make deliveries.

Let's use my bread business as an example. If a store placed an order directly with me, I would charge them a certain price which would include a delivery charge. The delivery charge didn't make me any money. I lost money because of the overhead. But, if they placed the order with an independent contractor, I would sell to the I.C. for a much lower price – my cost minus the overhead. The I.C. would then put his own price on the product, which included delivery and a small profit. The store would wind up paying the same price, but I saved money and the I.C. was able to make a decent living.

This is the deal I offered my drivers. The routes were priced at $60,000. I wanted $25,000 down. The balance I took as a note with a low weekly payment. If a driver needed to buy his truck, all he had to do was take over the payments. I didn't want to be paid for the vehicle.

If a route made $3,500-4,000 a week, a driver could make $1500 for himself. Even after paying on the loan and the truck, a driver could make $900-$1000 a week. If he grew the route, he could make a lot more. The only condition was that they had to buy their bread from me.

Here's a story that will make you laugh. I had a driver by the name of Tony. He had a habit of always grabbing his crotch when he walked. Every pair of jeans he owned was worn through in the area between his thigh and his crotch. I got so tired of seeing him that way, I bought him new clothes. He wore a toupee and always had a baseball cap on his head.

Tony drove a 16-foot Isuzu with a lift gate. It was a big truck... long. He was delivering on Atlantic Avenue in Delray Beach and got stopped at the red light near the railroad tracks. He was on the far side of the tracks with the rear of the truck up close to the rails. There was a Cadillac stopped at the light as well, right next to him.

The gates started to come down and the cars behind him... on the far side of the tracks, began beeping their horns. Tony got annoyed. He got out of the cab and walked to the rear of the truck. Since the gate was a half gate, it didn't reach to where the truck was parked. To Tony, it looked as if the truck was safe. He waved at the drivers behind him with his middle finger.

Yeah. Only the truck wasn't safe. The back end was only about a foot from the track, and Tony either forgot or never knew that a train is three feet wider than the rails on each side. When the train hit the truck, it lifted it into the air with the ease of a feather. When gravity pulled it back down, it landed on top of the Cadillac. Bread was everywhere.

Richie, my partner, called me and told me to turn on the news. We both thought Tony was dead. He was taken to Delray Medical Center. Richie and I got there as quickly as we could. In the meantime, I sent men to clean up the streets and throw away all the bread.

By some miracle, both Tony and the driver of the Cadillac were alive. Here's the funny part. Remember, the toupee. Tony had hit his head on the windshield and split open his skull. There was so much blood, the paramedics couldn't see all the damage. They thought his toupee was his real hair… that Tony had been scalped in the accident. When Richie and I got to his hospital room, the toupee was in a bowl surrounded by ice.

Early every morning I would be on the road in the hope of enticing new customers with free samples of our "diamonds." Diamonds were what I called the best breads in our line. These samples would have come out of the oven just a short time before so, they smelled and tasted delicious. The businesses I approached had been buying their bread from other vendors for years. I didn't really need to do a hard sell; our bread sold itself. One taste and they were hooked.

When our customer base had grown so big that I needed to lease a third bay, my dad came on board to help Anthony in the kitchen. With my dad and my brother doing the baking, I didn't have to worry about production.

People think the water in Florida isn't good for baking bread, but the water has little to do with it. Most bakeries take a beautiful loaf of bread and put it in a plastic bag. Big mistake. The bread gets soggy almost immediately.

We packaged our bread in brown paper bags. By doing this, we were able to keep the outside crispy and the inside soft and fluffy. Customers saw our bags and thought we were crazy. No one in Florida was doing it, but in New York, paper bag packaging was customary.

There were two reasons why our bread was better than anything being offered by our competitors. One was the packaging and the other was the way we mixed the ingredients. Old world bakers, like my dad, knew that there were special ingredients which would keep the bread tasting like it just came out of the oven. We only used the best.

As I've already said, our business was growing rapidly. Unfortunately, for us to grow, someone else's business had to fail. One day while I was making my rounds and dropping off samples, a guy pulled up beside my van. He got out and walked over to me. "Man," he said, "you're killing me."

"What do you mean I'm killing you. I don't even know you."

The guy explained, "You're taking all my stops. I've already lost five customers."

We began talking about the realities of the bakery business. He told me his name was Richie Hall and that he had a sizable customer base, but our breads were cutting into his profits. Richie wasn't a baker. He was the middle man; he bought bread from Protano's Bakery and then sold it to the customers along his routes.

Almost from the moment Richie approached me, I liked him. I could tell he was a hard worker; an honest man just trying to make a living. I was shocked when he told me that his wife had just died in an automobile accident, and he was raising his two kids alone – a daughter, 5, and a teen aged son. I estimated his age to be in his mid-thirties, and I knew he had a long road in front of him caring for his kids.

I'm a good judge of character, and Richie's story touched my heart.

I said, "Listen. Here's the deal. You buy bread from me, and I won't hit any of your customers. We can do great things together."

He agreed and, as it turned out, I was right. We became close friends and, eventually, partners in my bakery. Richie already had four trucks and four routes with 30-40 stops on each route. I had five trucks. We bought another truck together and by combining our stops, we had six or seven solid routes. We were doing over $21,000 a week in gross sales.

When the deal with Neil Schwartz died (I'll explain more about this shortly) and I was forced to close the bakery, Richie kept the routes and continued to sell through Romano's Bakery. That was 20 years ago. He's still selling bread, but now he buys it from a wholesale bakery in Fort Lauderdale.

Richie is the kind of guy who worries about everybody else. He always puts himself last. He's determined to get things done no matter what it takes. There aren't many people like him in this world. I truly appreciate him and value his friendship more than I can express in words.

CHAPTER THIRTY-ONE

With Dad and Anthony in charge of the baking and Richie now a part of our family, I was able to do what I did best – sell. I approached a supermarket chain with twelve locations. Cha-ching! One taste of our bread, and I walked away with a contract in hand.

Then, I went to a nearby restaurant. Just like in the old days, I went through the back door. The first person I met was Jose, the dishwasher. He told me everything I needed to know about the owner and the vendors. I noticed that the restaurant had bread baking equipment, so I asked to talk to the chef. He sampled our rolls and liked them a lot.

Suddenly, the manager walked into the kitchen. At first, he was hesitant to talk to me. I was a stranger, and I hadn't entered the restaurant the way most salesmen would have... through the front door and by appointment.

I'd played this game so many times before that I knew exactly what to do. With total sincerity, I apologized for disturbing the normal routine in the kitchen and explained why I was there. The chef had by this time become my biggest fan. He told the manager to taste the bread. More talking. Lots of laughing and another contract was signed and sealed. Every day more places opened accounts with us.

In six months, we had grown from one bay to five bays and were paying $1100 a month per bay. We needed a lot more equipment, which I bought at auction. Some of it needed to be repaired. I either did that myself or got help from my mechanic friends.

※

One day, a guy came into the warehouse offering to sell us three convection ovens. He had them on the back of a truck and was asking $20,000 a piece for them. Claimed they were in great shape.

Our mechanic checked them out. Two were perfect but the third was badly in need of work. I offered the guy $15,000 for all three, but he said "No." He left. Fifteen minutes later, he was back. He said, "Okay. I'll take $15,000 for the three ovens."

I didn't really need three ovens, so I told him, "I'll give you $10,000 for the two good ones. You keep the broken one." In the end, I gave him $12,000 for all three. The ovens were a legit buy… not hot off a truck.

※

To the hero line, we added Kaiser rolls and a few other varieties. We had no debt other than the cost of an ice machine, a hi lo oven and two mixers, which we leased. By now, we had 16 trucks. Everything was going well.

Right around this time, my brother-in-law, Tony, who had worked for Prudential Insurance in New York, decided to move to Florida. He took a job with Bank of America and asked if he could invest in the bakery. I thought that was a great idea.

Since all the equipment was owned outright except for those few pieces, Tony suggested we take loans against their value. He met with our accountant to put together an assessment of assets that would be the basis for the loan application.

Shortly thereafter, Dad got a phone call at the bakery. Some guy named Neil Swartz was trying to reach me. I had never heard of him, so I didn't rush to call him back. He kept calling. Said it was important.

When I had a few free minutes – there weren't many in those days – I called him. He told me his name was Neil Swartz and he wanted to buy my bakery. I was truly taken by surprise.

Neil said he ran *Z Bakery*, located on Palmetto Park and Powerline Roads in Boca Raton. *Z Bakery* made all the bread for *Zemi Restaurant*, a popular Boca establishment with high approval ratings. The bakery also had a sizable wholesale business.

I didn't know it at the time, but Dennis Kozlowski was also the primary investor in Zemi. There is a long, complicated story that involves Kozlowski and Mark Swartz, Neil's brother, being arrested for tax evasion to the tune of over a million bucks. All that was still to come as the Feds had not yet indicted the two men.

What I eventually learned was that Kozlowski had loaned John Belleme, Zemi's original owner and chef, $1.5 million to open the restaurant. Belleme's partners were Karen Mayo, Kozlowski's wife, and Allison Barber.

Confusing, right? Just imagine what it was like for me... a guy with no high school diploma and so dyslexic I struggled to read the Sunday comics.

To be honest, the deal Neil pitched to buy the bakery was enticing. I wasn't going to jump right in without talking to my dad and Tony but, since they both felt it was a dream come true, I gave him the thumbs-up.

Thinking back to my first meeting with Neil, I should have been suspicious. He had specifically stated that buying the bakery would be a personal investment for his corporation. However, everything from that first meeting forward seemed to be cloaked in double speak.

As I describe what came next, think Shark Tank. If you've never watched that show, do it now. It will make this story easier to understand.

The meeting was held in Neil's office in the Bank of America building in Boca Raton. Indirectly, I had a connection to that building. Tony worked for BOA in that location and the owner/manager of the building was Morris "Skip" Stoltz, President of Stoltz Companies and an old friend.

When I got to the meeting, Neil was there along with Howard Schiller, the company Controller. All the due diligence for buying my bakery had already been done. Howard had examined my assets and given the board his opinion on the pending deal. They probably knew my business better than I knew it.

Without any hesitation, they said they wanted to purchase the bakery and would get back to me shortly with an offer. Time passed. I was asked to go to another meeting at Neil's office. The conversation broke down to them saying that, while the bakery was worth the money I was asking, it was less valuable without me. I was, in their opinion, the bakery. Nice compliment... or not.

They offered to make me a partner in the overall venture – Z Bakery, South County Bakery (Delray Beach) and, of course, my own bakery. Since my place in Deerfield was big enough to house the entire operation, they planned to move all the equipment there and rename the business Z Bakery Wholesale. Just like that, three companies would morph into one.

CHAPTER THIRTY-TWO

We reached an agreement. I was going to have a 28% stake in the overall business, with a first payment of $100,000 when the deal was signed and $100,000 paid every three months until I had been fully compensated for the selling price of my bakery. Since my receivables were more than my payables, the board agreed to pay the rent, phone, gas and other expenses from the Corner Bakery profits, with the balance being paid to me as part of the deal. I was also getting a $500 car allowance and health insurance. My wife was pregnant at time, so the insurance sweetened the deal.

Two days before we were to sign the final contract, I got a call from Howard Schiller. He told me that, while the board still wanted to buy me out, they wanted to renegotiate the terms. I was livid! Furious, in fact. I know I said things I shouldn't have said. To Howard, they probably sounded like threats. Okay. They were threats... meaningless, but threats, nonetheless.

When I arrived at Neil's office, there were security guards and cops everywhere. All they knew was that someone had threatened Howard, but they didn't know who. Of course, once the guards and cops saw me... I knew everybody... they realized there was no real danger.

A few security people rode up to Neil's office in the elevator with me. Neil was waiting. I asked politely to speak with him. He said, "You threatened Howard." I said, "Let's talk." Neil told the guards that everything was "Okay," and they could leave.

We began to discuss our differences of opinion. Neil said that the board had decided to spread out my payments over four years. He also said that they were going to renegotiate all my corporate accounts – receivables and payables. They would still use my receivables to pay the bills, but all decisions from this point forward would be theirs to make. I was so naïve. I just wanted everything paid and the extra time didn't seem like a big deal.

Here's where Shark Tank comes in.

My vendors were given two choices. They could either be paid in full but no longer do business with *Z Bakery*, or they could settle for half what they were owed and continue to be a vendor. The board used the hook that they were putting three bakeries together into one huge operation to lure them in. The vendors didn't have any choice. They all signed off on the debt.

Neil made a fortune. The receivables remained the same but with only half the payouts. I was truly amazed that they had finagled such a great deal for themselves.

So, now we're partners, and the business is doing well. Rosario Jr. is born and the insurance covers everything. Think pig in shit. I was pulling a weekly salary and was also in charge of turning *Z Bakery* into a café type place with artisan breads of my own design. That venture was so successful we talked about opening more cafes up and down the east coast.

Slowly, troubles started to plague the operation. The phones were still in my name; a violation of our contract but one I didn't think to question. South County Bakery was moved to my place in Deerfield, and the move proved to be much more expensive than anticipated.

Money suddenly got tight. Investors began pulling out, and Neil began taking money out of the *Corner Bakery* and *Z Bakery* accounts to keep his operation afloat. If not for the papers and evening news, I would never have known what was happening. The Feds were quickly closing in on the Swartz brothers and Kozlowski. I was caught completely off guard.

In a desperate attempt to salvage the operation, Neil brought in a guy by the name of John Carlo. He tried to pass him off as an Italian – as if that would make him more appealing to me – but he was Venezuelan. John was supposed to be a new investor. His job was to oversee all the accounts.

Neil gave John an office in the BOA building. I went there to meet him, and right from the introduction, I knew something he was shady. He carried a gun; made sure that everyone saw it; and joked about how he would use it if things didn't go his way. He thought he was a big shot and the gun gave him power. That's never a good sign.

It was a habit for me to stop by Neil's office every week to pick up my check. One day, I ran into Skip Stoltz, who told me that Neil hadn't paid the rent in five months. I said I would investigate and get back to him.

When I asked Neil why he was behind in the rent, he said that he was in a bind and was going to use my money to pay Skip. I could see he was desperate, but I didn't care. Based on the terms of our original deal, he owed Richie and me over $300,000, including pay, car payments, and insurance. He refused to give me a check.

A few days later, I started getting phone calls from the route drivers. They had been calling the bakery only to learn that the phones had been shut off. It was early in the morning… before normal business hours… so, there was no way for me to find out what was going on. What I did know was that if the corporate accounts called the office and got no answer, they would take their business elsewhere. I couldn't let that happen.

When the bank opened, I took $1200 from my personal account and paid the phone bill in person. The phones were back on within minutes. Now, I not only wanted to know what was happening, I wanted the money I had given to the phone company back. I drove directly to Neil's office.

While parking my car, I saw a locksmith's truck in the lot. Upstairs, the locks on all the doors were being changed on John's orders. This had nothing to do with me but resulted from so many poor decisions being made by company executives. The Feds were getting closer, and I was still in the dark. I asked John for a key because my business records were in the office. He refused to give me one. He also refused to reimburse me for the phone bill.

By now you know that I have what could be described as a volatile personality. John and I started arguing. I told him to pay me for the phone bill, or I would go back to the phone company and have the phones shut off. I had a pen in my hand when I said this and, I guess, he thought I was going to stab him. I wasn't, but he called Neil to say he was scared. Neil told him to pay me.

What followed was another eye opener. John went down to the parking lot and took a wad of cash out of his trunk. I asked him about the back pay that was owed to me, but he said he didn't have that kind of money. From what I saw in the trunk, he did.

Even though the bills at the bakery were still being paid, I knew the writing was on the wall. Trouble was brewing, and I needed to do something to save myself and what was left of my reputation.

Needless to say, I was furious. I had worked hard to build up *Z Bakery* and the overall business accounts, but now, because of the Swartz/Kozlowski debacle, I had to get out. No one told me to get out. I just knew it was the right thing to do.

I walked away from everything -- my bakery, my investment, the money I was owed -- everything that I had worked for was gone in the blink of an eye.

CHAPTER THIRTY-THREE

I admit to having a quick temper, but I'm also quick to recover from whatever misfortunes threaten to bring me down. With the bread deal down the toilet, I couldn't afford not to work, so I looked around for a new opportunity.

In the same commerce park where the bakery was located, there was a kosher deli. The business was struggling, and the owner badly wanted to sell. I offered to buy him out at a reduced price but keep him on as a silent partner. Nothing would change other than I would be supplying the bread and running the business behind the scenes. We would start small and build from there. He agreed.

Again, I went into salesman mode. There was a real estate school across the street, and the students were prone to frequenting a nearby IHOP. Not for long. Once they tasted what we had to offer, they became steady customers.

Angelo came over every morning and hung out with his buddies. While he knew his way around a counter, he was already 80 years old and didn't really want to work hard. The deli was perfect for him.

I'm sure you are all familiar with the name John Gotti. Nicknamed the Teflon Don, Gotti's reach as the boss of the Gambino crime family was far and wide. At the peak of his power, he was considered one of the most dangerous criminals in the country.

In 1984, while living in New York, John Gurino, Jr. was acquitted of the drive-by killing of John Vulcano. Why he killed him, I don't know, but why Gurino went free is easy to figure out. His lawyer was Bruce Cutler, a very clever attorney who eventually became the Gambino family lawyer while Gotti was in charge.

While representing Gurino in the murder of Vulcano, Cutler filled the courtroom with men whose appearance alone labeled them mob connected. Each day a caravan of Lincoln Town Cars bearing Boca Raton, Florida license plates would pull up in front of the courthouse. Twenty-five to 30 men would take their seats in the gallery, sitting in quiet intimidation of all who saw them. Volcano's girlfriend had been scheduled to testify but, one look at those men, and she rescinded her testimony. Even though Vulcano had named Gurino as his killer with his dying breath, the jury found him not guilty.

In 1992, when John Gotti was found guilty of five murders, conspiracy to commit murder, loan sharking, illegal gambling, obstruction of justice, bribery and tax evasion, John Gurino, Jr. led a crowd of over 1,000 supporters, who protested in front of the federal courthouse in Brooklyn. The crowd, encouraged by Gurino who continually agitated them using a bullhorn, caused extensive damage and injuries to police officers. Gurino was charged with numerous felonies.

In 2001, Peter Zacarro was approached by Big Tony Moscatiello with a contract to kill Gus Boulis. He was already gainfully employed so he offered the contract to his good friend John Gurino, Jr. What followed is the reason for this book.

Gurino started coming into the store and pestering Angelo to make changes. He suggested turning the place into a newsstand -adding cigarettes, cigars, magazines – stuff like that. Angelo said he was just helping me out. It wasn't his place to make any decisions about the business.

Gurino didn't give up. He offered to buy out Angelo's share and put his son in as my partner. I thought it was a good idea. It wasn't.

CHAPTER THIRTY-FOUR

If not for the bakery situation, I would never have considered getting into a partnership with John Gurino. There had always been rumors about his "associates," but nothing had ever been proven.

While I was pretty much debt free on the bakery, I wasn't quite so solid personally. My wife and I were building a big house and the bills were piling up. One day, we were at the site of our future home when a guy showed up in a landscaping truck and introduced himself as "JJ" (John Gurino). Although I knew his family, I had never met him before this day. The meeting seemed like a coincidence but, now that I have the benefit of hindsight, I can see that it wasn't.

One day, John and I went to an equipment store to buy a grill. There were a lot of Jewish businesses in the area, and it seemed wise to offer some hot foods and ethnic items like knishes. I didn't have enough ready cash to pay for the grill so, even though I hated having more debt, John charged it to his credit card.

Three days later, Angelo called me. He said that John had shown up with a truck and removed the chicken rotisserie and some other equipment. He brought in a hot dog grill and a steam table. I knew nothing about it. When I questioned John, he said it was equipment we didn't use but that he had stored it where it would be safe.

Angelo was spitting nails. He hadn't been paid for the business and John was removing equipment and making lots of changes. I told him he needed to pay Angelo what was owed to him, but John didn't think it was a big deal. He promised to pay him when all the renovations had been made.

John kept pushing for more changes. He would intentionally come in during the heavy lunch hour rush and start talking about doing this and that. I couldn't discuss business while people were ordering corned beef and coleslaw. I was reaching the end of my rope.

There came a day when, right around the noon hour, he arrived at the deli and began to shout orders at me. The lunch time crowd was out the door and he wanted me to put up a potato chip rack. I told him to wait until everyone had been served. He went nuts. It took all my self-control to remain calm while calming him down.

John's son, for whom he supposedly bought into the deli, was slow to start working. We talked about when he would begin and settled on a date. The kid showed up; looked around and walked out. We never saw him again.

The very next day, John cornered Angelo at the deli and told him that, since his son had no interest in working there, he wanted to be paid for the equipment he had brought in and the changes he had made. Angelo asked, "Pay you for what? You took my equipment out. Bring it back and take yours. I don't owe you anything." John refused to leave.

Again, Angelo was furious. He called me and demanded that I get to the store asap. I went. When I got there, I asked John what was going on. He said, "You gotta pay me for all this equipment, and you better fucking pay me now."

I admit I was surprised. Never expected any of this to happen. I told him to "Just take back what's yours. If you don't, I'll put it out in the parking lot tomorrow morning and you can pick it up."

We were two ticking time bombs waiting to explode. The situation quickly went from bad to worse.

CHAPTER THIRTY-FIVE

Killing John Gurino had far reaching effects and not in the ways most people would expect.

On the favorable side, I'm slower to anger these days. I'm not only older biologically than when I went to prison in 2005, I'm wiser. There's a big difference between being smart and being wise. I was always smart; now, wise gets me through some tough days.

While now I think before I act, I still have no patience for stupidity. I met so many people in prison who were out and out dumb. Seriously, when the brain was forming in the womb, they must have been absent without leave. There is no other way to describe their inability to solve even the simplest of problems. I was never what you would call naïve, but after 12 years behind bars, I realized that there are some people who should never be on the outside. Not because they were innately bad. They just were, well, stupid.

For example, there was this young kid who slept in the bottom bunk of a cell we shared. He weighed about 300 pounds. One day, I came back to the cell after being out in the recreation yard. I was hot and sweaty; all I wanted to do was rest.

Much to my unbelieving eyes, I found my cellmate sitting on the toilet while eating a hamburger and potato chips. He was holding a can of soda between his knees. The sight of him left me speechless for a minute.

Once my brain had accepted what my eyes were seeing, I had all I could do to control myself. He should have eaten his meal in the cafeteria and stunk up one of the general use toilets. I told him to get done and get out as I wanted to lay down. He said he needed more time. I could hear and smell his crap as it fell into the toilet and it was nauseating.

I was ready for a fight, but you really can't fight with a guy when his ass is sitting on the can. I asked him, "Do you know that what you're doing is disgusting? What's wrong with you? Are you afraid that you'll starve if you don't replace what you already digested with more food? Does your stomach need to be full 24 hours a day?"

The guy knew he was in a compromising position, so he just mumbled an answer. I left. There was no way I was going to get any sleep with him providing sound effects.

It didn't get any better as the day wore on. I had the top bunk and, since smells are intensified by heat and humidity (the cell was an oven) and the guy farted all night, well, you can just imagine.

It drives me crazy to listen to people preach about things they know nothing about; and thanks to the internet, everyone thinks they know everything about everything. These are the same people who require an hour and a half to understand what was reported on *60 Minutes*.

Before prison, I never relied on anyone but myself. Now, my wife is my life line. When I feel tension rising, I call her no matter where I am. When I first got out of jail, I was driving a truck to make some money. As a felon, I couldn't get life insurance and the bills had piled up while I was away. I needed to work.

Free just two weeks, I was driving south on the I-95 when a guy cut me off and almost caused me to have an accident. I was *this* close to being dead or seriously injured. I felt my blood start to boil.

Even though I knew I shouldn't, I followed the guy into a bank parking lot. Thankfully, my wife called just as I was opening the truck door. She calmed me down. Man, do I ever love her!

One thing I know for sure… time is precious.

I was just a kid when my dad got arrested in the Operation Doughboy sting. It was traumatic; left me afraid of breaking the law in any way. I never even got a speeding ticket; always kept my nose clean. If a business venture appeared to be a bad risk legally, I steered away from it. That's why my involvement with John Gurino and its ultimate outcome took me by surprise.

John was a vulture. Of course, I didn't know he was a vulture until it was too late. When he first appeared on the scene, it was to buy lunch at the deli. If I was there, we'd talk. We got friendly, and I told him about how the failure of the Neil Schwartz/Tyco deal had put me in a tough spot financially.

My wife and I had been building a house prior to that fiasco and I was over my head in mortgage payments. There were two loans, and when Z Bakery went under, my credit rating hit rock bottom. I was under a lot of pressure and my morale was at an all-time low.

John offered to help me out. At first, I said "No." I was in no position to owe someone else money. Time passed, and John offered again. By now, I had met his wife and kids, and everyone seemed nice. I began to wonder if I had misread his intentions. When the wolf is at your door, it's never a good time to make decisions without knowing all the facts. I was a fool.

When I was down to my last few dollars, John once again offered to help me out. I said, "Okay. Maybe just a few thousand."

Truthfully, I was grateful; I thought he really cared. I never expected to be abused by him.

As I've already written, the situation quickly went from bad to worse. John began making threats… saying things like, "Pay me, or you're gonna feel warm blood pouring down your arm." It was as if that old sci-fi television series, *Lost in Space*, was playing in my head. I kept hearing a robotic voice saying, "Danger Rosario!"

CHAPTER THIRTY-SIX

No one needed to tell me to change the locks at the deli. I smiled while it was being done, remembering how I had felt when John Carlo had changed the locks at Tyco. I had gotten annoyed that he wouldn't give me a key, and I was pretty sure Gurino would be just as annoyed. I wasn't wrong.

The first incident happened during a very busy lunch rush. My mom was working the register. Gurino got up close to her face and whispered in her ear, "You're in a lot of trouble. It's just a matter of time." I saw him talking to my mom, but I couldn't hear what he was saying because I was waiting on a customer. As soon as I was finished, I started to walk over to him. That's when I heard something metallic hit the floor. Neither mom nor I saw what it was because Gurino grabbed it and put it in his pocket. He quickly left. That's when a customer told us Gurino had a gun.

Another night, mom was at the deli until closing – around 8 pm. My wife would often help my mom when she worked late, but on this night, she was home with the baby. I was behind the counter; mom was on the customer side. We saw Gurino pull into the parking lot.

I've legally owned guns since I was in my early twenties, but I rarely carried them on my person. With Gurino threatening carnage, I had put one of my guns in a briefcase and stored it under the counter. It wasn't easily accessible, but I felt safer.

I went to the door and blocked Gurino from entering. We started arguing. I told my mom to go home, but she refused. I kept yelling at her to "Get out!" but she wouldn't leave me alone with what was becoming a life-threatening situation.

Gurino started cursing and trying to get his hands on me, but my mom was in his way. She kept putting herself between us, trying to break up the fight. Mom weighed about 105 pounds; she was a little thing, and Gurino pushed her hard. He hurt her, but still she wouldn't leave.

Instead, she took out her cell phone and dialed 911. Unfortunately, she never hit *Send*, but Gurino didn't know that. He took off in his SUV, yelling, "I'll get you!"

This all happened about two weeks before our final confrontation. Had mom called 911... had the police had a record of Gurino's behavior... I would never have been charged with murder in his death. At least, that's what the cops told me. The prosecutor had big dreams and being my greatest nightmare was one of them.

Things were quiet for about two weeks. Then, one morning while I am collecting our mail, Gurino drove up. The shopping center where the deli was located did not have delivery directly to individual businesses. This was a cluster mailbox type of situation; the mailboxes were set apart from the stores and hidden behind a five-foot hedge, effectively making someone getting their mail invisible to passersby.

I had parked my car so that the driver's door was closest to the mailboxes. If not for needing to unlock the box, I could have reached through the driver's window and gotten my mail without getting out of the car. My gun was in the glove compartment. Never thought I would need it.

Gurino pulled his car up close to mine, essentially making a "T" with our two vehicles. In other words, he parked with the front end of his car touching my passenger side door. Another car with three or four guys inside pulled up close to my trunk and tightly boxed me in.

Gurino jumped out of his car, holding his hand behind his back. He said something like, "Now, they know what you look like," and he nodded to the knuckle walkers in the other car.

There really was no way for me to defend myself unless they got close enough for me to kick them in the balls. I was wearing construction boots with steel tips. Since I didn't think that was going to happen, I took a position of total defiance. I dared them to come and get me.

"Come on! Now that you know what I look like, why wait. Do it now. Kill me." With that, I walked over and kicked in the passenger door of their car. Nobody moved. They didn't so much as crack open the window.

Then, I pointed at Gurino. "Now, you're the guy. You're after me? No. I'm after you."

I was practically climbing over the roof of my car to get to him. There was a busy gas station a short distance away; I kept hoping the people there would hear the commotion and call the police.

I saw that Gurino was holding a gun at his side. He challenged me, "You got your gun? You gonna shoot me?"

I wouldn't back down. "I got no gun. You got the gun." Again, I was shouting, hoping the people at the gas station would hear me.

Gurino got back into his car and started to pull away. I ran after him; he saw me in the rearview mirror, backed up and tried to run over me.

Again, he pulled away. I got into my car and chased him. The guys in the other car were long gone. By the time I pulled out of the shopping center, Gurino was nowhere to be seen.

I was so mad, I couldn't think straight. I drove to his house. He lived in a gated community, but since I had been there so often, the guard just let me through. Never called up to the house for permission.

Gurino's car was parked in the driveway. I walked up to the door and knocked. At trial, this behavior would be depicted as "aggressive" and used against me by the prosecutor, but at that moment, I just wanted the whole situation to be over.

From outside, I could hear Gurino yelling at his wife not to let me in. He kept telling her to "Get away from the door!" I could hear his footsteps on the tile floor, and I saw his shadow through the frosted glass panel. Without opening the door, he asked, "Whatta you want?"

I said, "Come on out. Let's get this over with."

He had the advantage; he could have shot me right then and there. I don't know why he didn't. Maybe he didn't want to get blood on his fancy flooring. I kept asking him to come outside, so we could talk, but he wouldn't leave the safety of his home. I left.

CHAPTER THIRTY-SEVEN

Aggressive behavior. That's how the prosecutor explained my inclination to chase Gurino after he threatened my life in the parking lot. Seriously, what did this schmuck expect me to do? Go home, pop open a beer and watch a football game?

No one I know walks away from a direct threat on their life. Doing so would be an open invitation to come back and follow through on the threat. I was raised to protect myself and my family by whatever means necessary. Despite my temper, I have never been a violent man. Don't even like guns, but I've always had one because delivery guys are easy targets for crooks.

I don't go looking for trouble. Whenever possible, I will talk my way out of a situation. Words have always been my best weapons in times of trouble.

~

It's common knowledge that back in the day you couldn't be in the food service industry without meeting members of one crime family or another. Many of them lived in the south end of Palm Beach County, especially in the area where the bakery was located. I had a lot of admiration for the old goombas. They were smart men; men who grew up poor but build an empire from which they were now comfortably retired.

Ask any Italian and he or she will tell you that we tend to gravitate to each other. Italian doctors, Italian contractors, Italian restaurants -- we just feel more comfortable among our own kind. So, it was no surprise that the old guard would frequent my store. I enjoyed their company; listening to their stories was always an education. I never charged them for anything. It was a matter of respect.

One morning, I got a phone call from the bakery bookkeeper. She told me that there six men at the office waiting to see me. I had her put one of them on the phone. A few seconds later, I heard Angelo's voice. He said the men wanted to talk to me and asked me to meet them at the Clock Restaurant. I agreed although I had no idea what they wanted.

When I got to the restaurant, it was like stepping into a scene from the Sopranos. The six men, all in their sixties, wearing lots of gold chains and heavy gold rings, were sitting around a table drinking coffee. None of them were sitting with their back to the door or window. They were too smart for that. There was a new guy with them; someone I had never met before.

Angelo introduced the new guy, who seemed to be in charge, as Bruno. Bruno said that they all wanted to go into partnership with me. Now, when these men use the word "want," they aren't making a polite request. If you understand their language, you know it's a command… just not to me.

I told them that I didn't need any more partners as I'd already done all the work in building the business. They countered by saying that they could provide me with 40-50 additional stops – customers along my route. Bruno told a guy who was sitting at a nearby table to "… get the bag out of the car." The bag was full of money.

Again, I told them I didn't need partners, but I didn't want to shut them down completely for fear of retribution. I made them a counter offer.

"Let's say you bring me a customer who places a $500 order for bread. After two months, I'll give you $500 to buy the stop from you –

a finder's fee. I'll do that for every customer you bring me." They were quick to agree.

Within a month, the old guys brought me 20 accounts. Sixteen of them never paid their bills and the others… their checks bounced. I was determined to collect every penny that was owed to me.

I remember this one restaurant on Clematis Street. It was a nice place – expensive. The owner was a sharp dresser – mafia style. When I met him, he said he wanted to order ciabatta bread for his grand opening. I gave him a price of $200 for 50 loaves. He felt the price was too high even after I offered to throw in a week of bread for free.

We found common ground, and I placed his order. His checks bounced – every one of them. Finally, I told my driver "No money when you deliver, no bread. Leave it on the truck until the cash is in your hand." The driver was afraid of the restaurant guy and for good reason. There was no mistaking that he was the dangerous sort.

Finally, I got tired of not being paid and told him to buy his bread from somebody else. He didn't like being cornered and promised to pay. I knew better than to believe him, so I said that I would deliver his bread daily. "Pay me… you get your bread. Don't pay me… I leave with your bread."

He accused me of holding his bread hostage. I told him it wasn't his bread until he paid for it. He was furious, but he did pay me. As I left, I told him he had just had his last delivery.

There was another restaurant guy whose checks never cleared. It was Christmas time and my bills were running high. I needed to be paid so I could pay my workers and my suppliers. I went to see him and told him I wouldn't deliver any more orders until he covered his debt. He gave me a third-party check for $400. It bounced! I told him to start buying his bread at Publix.

He was so angry, he followed me out to my car, yelling the whole way. He saw the CL 600 Mercedes I was driving and began to bust my chops, saying I needed his money to pay for my wheels. I had enough.

There was no other choice but to cut him off, which I did, but I was determined to get what he owed me. I arranged with a friend of mine to book a party for 15 people at the restaurant. All he had to do was call me when the bill arrived at his table and I would take care of it. He did just that.

As soon as I got the call, I went to the restaurant, looked over the bill, signed it and gave the waitress a $100 tip. Then, I told the owner to deduct the bill from what he owed me. He called the police. The cops said it was a civil matter, and I still had to pay for the party. I charged it on my American Express card.

When my monthly statement came in the mail, I called Amex and told them that somebody must have stolen my card. The signature on the bill wasn't mine. They believed me. Drove that restaurant guy crazy. He should have just paid me what was due on his account.

There was a third guy… owned a small deli. His checks were made of rubber. I took 10 cases of soda out of his store while he just stood there and watched. I considered his debt paid in full.

Finally, I called the old guard and asked them to meet me at the Clock Restaurant. I showed them the unpaid accounts and told them that they owed me $3500. Then, I said that if they could collect the money, it was theirs to keep. A gift from me to them. We shook hands; I said, "Ciao," and was glad to never see them again.

CHAPTER THIRTY-EIGHT

Because of how the FBI had treated my father, the way they had ransacked our house and made my mother cry, I was determined that I would keep my nose clean. At the time of Gurino's death, I had had a concealed carry permit for more than 30 years. The gun was a necessary evil.

There was this one time while making a delivery to a D'Agostino store in New York, a thief looking for an easy mark, which I was, put a box cutter to my throat and demanded money. He didn't even wait for me to reach for my wallet. Just ripped open the pocket of my pants with the box cutter and took it.

Many of the deliveries I made were hazardous because of how they had to be done. In some cases, I would pull the truck over behind the store, empty the goods and bring them inside. Then, I would move the truck. Often, that meant parking a distance away so as to leave room for the next delivery guy. Walking back to the store made me an irresistible target. A lot of places paid in cash.

When I was a kid, my dad had two jobs – milkman in the morning and taxi cab driver in the evening. My parents had bought a house on Long Island, trying to give my siblings and me a home of our own. Two jobs barely covered expenses.

I remember watching my father come home in the wee hours of the morning, exhausted from driving the cab all night. He would barely fall asleep when it was time to get up and deliver the milk. Some days, I would do the deliveries with him.

We had an old car at the time. I can't remember the make or model, but I do know the car was small. I was 12 or 13 - long before I could legally drive a car. Anyway, I would go to work with dad and when he finished his route, I would steer that little car home. He would be out cold behind the wheel. My driving was erratic – all stop and go. Since dad was in the driver's seat, I would have to lean over him to steer and hit the brakes. He rarely woke up until I nudged him and said we were back at the house.

To help make ends meet, my parents took in a tenant. I can't remember her name, but she had a granddaughter whom I remember well. Her name was Sandy. What a crush I had on her!

One day, when I was out with dad on his milk run, I saw a sign for a go kart for sale. We didn't have the money to buy it, but dad saw the look on my face and knew what was in my heart. Somehow, he found a way.

The day he gave it to me… that was one of the best days of my life. First thing I did was write "Sandy" on the side. I don't know if she ever noticed; she never said anything, but I was so proud to ride that kart around the neighborhood. Still makes me smile to think about it.

I grew up believing that dreams do come true. Making them come true requires hard work, but that always seemed like the reward for a job well done. That's why the events that led up to me going to jail were such a surprise to me.

Before the shit hit the fan, Gurino offered to buy the dream house my wife and I were building. Because of Neil and Tyco, I was in over my head; we could no longer afford to continue with the construction. Since it's almost impossible to sell a house pre-construction, Gurino's offer seemed like a godsend.

He went to an attorney and had a contract drawn up. It looked good on the surface. I thought I would be able to get my $150,000 down payment back, which would help to pay off our mounting bills.

When I read the contract, I saw that Gurino had stated that he put down a payment of $50,000. That was just an *on paper* deposit. He hadn't put down any money, claiming that the pretend deposit was meant to cover what he was owed through the business. I told him he was nuts. At max, he was owed $11,000. I refused to sign the contract.

Gurino was furious. We exchanged words and the situation got heated. Not physical. Just words. This happened before the mailbox incident and was, probably, the reason for that confrontation.

If I had had a crystal ball, I still would not have believed what happened next. Two or three days after Gurino refused to come out of his house – the day of the mailbox incident – he called my cell phone.

"You at the house?" (He meant the house under construction.)

"Yeah."

"Mom and baby?"

"Yeah."

"I'm coming over."

There was no way I was letting him near my family. I told him that I would meet him some other place.

He said, "No. I'm coming to your house and I'm bringing some guys. We're gonna rape you in front of your wife and son."

He wasn't talking about Rosario, Jr., who was just an infant. He was referring to my 11-year-old son Jimmy. I pretended not to be concerned, but when I hung up the phone, I called my mom. Told her she needed to come quickly to pick up Jimmy and the baby and take them to her house.

Once they were gone, I went outside and hid behind some dumpsters where Gurino couldn't see me, but I could see him. I waited… and waited. He never showed up.

A few days later, there was a voicemail on my phone. He was at the new house and the garage door opener wouldn't work. I had disconnected it once our deal fell through. Again, he made threats, which the cops heard after the shooting, but it was too late to help my case.

CHAPTER THIRTY-NINE

The morning Gurino died started out just like every other morning. I usually ran errands, and on this day, I was at the restaurant depot picking up some things that were needed in the deli kitchen. My mom and Peter, the young man who became a defense witness at my trial, always met at the store and did the prep work for the lunch crowd. Peter had worked for the previous owner of the deli and had great references. I trusted him.

Shortly after Peter arrived, at approximately 8 am, Gurino came in, ranting that he was in charge.

To say that Peter was frightened would be an understatement. He had long been wary of Gurino, never wanting to be alone in his presence. He left the store, went to a nearby gas station and called me on my cell phone. I immediately called my mom and told her not to go to work. Then, I called Angelo and told him to meet me at the deli.

When I arrived at the store, no one was there. I locked the door and waited for Angelo to arrive. Because of Gurino's earlier threats, I had started carrying a gun in my briefcase. I took that gun and put it on a shelf behind the cold cut slicer. It was out of sight but easily reachable should trouble arise. I had also taken the precaution of sending my wife and infant son to Georgia to keep them safe.

In the meantime, my mom ignored my warning and set out to find Peter at the gas station. She, too, called my cell phone to tell me that the two of them were sitting outside in her car just in case I needed help. She also said that they could see Gurino eating breakfast at the nearby pancake house. He was not alone.

I shut the lights and went about setting up the coffee and doing the prep work that Mom and Peter would have done. I kept myself busy, but I was ever watchful knowing that Gurino could pound on the door at any minute, which he did. Through the glass panel, I could see his brightly patterned Hawaiian shirt and a .38 Smith and Wesson revolver sticking out from the waistband of his pants.

When he realized the door was locked and I wasn't going to open it, he started screaming that he was taking control of everything... the store, my house, my life. Three or four times he made the trip from the front door of the deli to his truck, then to the pancake house and back to the deli, getting madder with each trip.

During one of his absences, my mom called to say that Angelo had arrived, and he had another guy, Augie, with him. Feeling safer now that I had backup, I unlocked the door.

Gurino must have seen Angelo and Augie from the restaurant because no sooner had they stepped inside, then he was back. This time he brought a friend - Bobby. Bobby was well past 70 and fat. He could barely move and needed two elbow crutches just to walk a short distance.

When Gurino entered the deli, he appeared calm. He and Bobby walked past me as though I wasn't even there. They walked to the rear of the restaurant where Angelo and Augie were sitting at a table. The dining area for the deli's customers was long and narrow. There was no back door. Only one way in and one way out. Gurino took a seat with his back to the front door.

Calm is not how I would ever describe Gurino's demeanor. The fact that he ignored me was disconcerting. I wasn't scared for me, but I was worried about my friends. I knew in my heart that a resolution needed to be reached, and it could not wait another day. Whatever it took, the terror that Gurino had inflicted on me, my family, my employees... it had to end.

I continued setting up for the day's business. Gurino called to me; asked me to join them at the table. I sat backward on one of the chairs prepared to move quickly if the need arose.

We began to talk. No, that's not true. I talked; he shouted. The former calm had disappeared. Aware of what he was capable of doing, I told him I would pay him $50,000 as soon as I sold my house.

Fifty thousand dollars was a lot more than he was owed. He should have been happy, but the mention of the money triggered something in him. When I said, "Now, it's over," his response was "Nothing's over."

It was my turn to ignore him. I finished setting up for our soon-to-arrive customers. As I was working near the deli counter, Gurino took a swing at my face. Luckily, I saw him coming and pulled my head away. Then, I saw his hand reach for the waist of his khaki slacks. He was trying to remove something that was stuck in the pocket.

I remembered seeing the gun and, with no time to lose, ran around the counter and grabbed my gun. I hadn't thought to put a bullet in the chamber, so I had to cock it and in doing so, I released four shots. I hadn't even taken aim. The gun just went off.

The first shot hit Gurino in his right nipple. He spun around, and the next two shots hit him in the back and the buttocks. He began to crawl toward the door. One of the shots had gone wild, shattering the glass panel into a thousand pieces. The glass covered him like a blanket as he tried to crawl away. By that time, he was half in and half out of the doorway.

When I reached for my gun, I was in survival mode. Afterward, I was in shock. I kept staring at Gurino saying, "You did this. Not me. You ruined my life and your life."

Not to be funny but my so-called backup and Gurino's friend Bobby took off at the sound of the first shot. By some miracle, Bobby was able to run out of the deli without the use of his crutches. They stepped right over Gurino as they made their escape. To be fair, Angelo put his fears aside and testified to everything he had seen and heard at my trial.

A crowd gathered outside the store. Mostly, they were customers from the pancake house. Some people tried to help Gurino. They got towels and tried to stop the blood while waiting for the paramedics. Luckily, no one had been injured by the wild bullet. Had that happened, I don't think I could ever forgive myself.

People kept shouting for me to do something, but I truly didn't know what to do. The man had threatened to rape me in front of my wife and son; he had threatened to murder me. I was angry and, yet, I was filled with sorrow. I knew his family… his wife and kids. I was so sad for them.

This wasn't the first time I had fired a gun, but it was the first time I had killed someone. There's a big difference between attending a funeral and seeing a dead body on your doorstep.

I called 911 and explained what had happened. The person who took the call told me to stay calm. She asked where the weapon was, and I told her it was in a safe place.

Then, I called my mom, who was still in the parking lot, and told her she was safe. I also called my dad and told him to find me a lawyer even though I knew I wasn't guilty of any wrong doing. Finally, I went to the kitchen to wait for the police and think about what the future would hold. I was confident no one would see me as the aggressor and that the case would be quickly resolved.

CHAPTER FORTY

Very soon the parking lot was filled with law enforcement vehicles. There were cops from the Boca Raton police department, Sheriff's Office deputies, homicide detectives and assorted other uniformed personnel. Once they had secured the premises and taken possession of my gun, they were very respectful. I was never handcuffed or treated roughly. They all believed that the shooting had been a case of self-defense.

While I was being questioned, the paramedics tried to revive Gurino, but it was too late. He was declared dead at the scene and his body taken to the coroner's office for whatever they do in a case like this.

Sitting at one of the tables in the back of the deli, I got hungry. A cop had been stationed nearby to keep an eye on me. Hours passed, and my stomach started growling.

I asked the cop, "Hey, could you grab me a sandwich and a soda from the case?" He said, "I don't think it's a good idea for you to be eating right now."

I was thinking that I could be going to jail for life and this could be my last meal, so I just got up, grabbed a bag of chips and a Snapple and sat back down. As far as I knew, that wasn't a crime.

My wife had a habit of buying me tee shirts with silly sayings. On the day Gurino died, I was wearing one that read, "He who enters here might not leave," or something like that. The sheriff who was taking me to the precinct saw the shirt and shook his head as if to say, "Bad idea."

What he did say was, "Buddy, you gotta do something about that shirt. Turn it inside out." I never realized how damning what was written could be, so I appreciated his concern for me.

Once the crime scene was secured, the cops roped off the parking lot. Angelo, Augie and Bobby were long gone. Everyone else had to be cleared before they could get in their car and leave. Once all the bystanders were gone, the remaining vehicles were towed – Angelo's car, mine and Gurino's were included.

Two days later, I went to the precinct to claim my car. The detective on my case said he wanted to swab my mouth. I didn't know what to do so I quickly called my lawyer (the attorney from Coral Gables) and told him. He asked me if I had anything to worry about, which I didn't. He said, "Let him do it."

Getting my car back required the signing of a release which gave the police permission to search it before I took ownership. I was okay with that. I went to the tow lot where the car was being held and saw it completely covered in crime scene tape... the doors, the trunk... everything. I watched as a crime scene van pulled up and a technician went from door to door and carefully cut each piece of tape, photographing everything as she methodically searched the vehicle.

Among the items she found were three more firearms... a .32, a Beretta, and a 9mm. She also found two loose bullets. To this day, I don't know how that could have happened. I never loaded a gun in the car, and I was never careless. I have a lot of respect for guns.

Other people did occasionally drive the car so, maybe, my son or someone else touched the bullets. No one ever admitted to it. There was cash in an envelope in the glove compartment as well, but the police left that alone.

Even though the guns were legally owned, they were confiscated. I never got them back. I have no idea what became of them. My guess is they were destroyed.

∼

When I was finally arrested, I was forbidden to have a gun. I also could not drink, leave Palm Beach County or have any contact with Gurino's family. Once I was under investigation for murder, the cops behaved like pit bulls fighting over one bone. To say they were persistent would be an understatement.

∼

When the crime scene techs were finished collecting evidence, the original owner of the deli came back and cleaned the place up. On paper, he was still the proprietor.

At the time I bought the store, we made a deal that we never discussed with anyone else. I gave him $50,000. He kept the license in his name. The name on the front door was different, but the name on the license remained the same.

I'm sure you are wondering why I did that. Because of the screwing I got from Neil in the bakery deal, I was afraid the leasing company would hold that failed business venture against me. It could take years before I was approved to rent property or hold a business license.

Many Italians believe in a superstition called the malocchio or evil eye. The evil eye is a look that one person gives another to cause them harm whether out of envy, jealousy, or some imagined slight. I didn't believe in any of that old-world stuff, but to be honest, I was wishing I had hung a horn (to ward off bad luck) over the door. Eventually, the deli was sold to someone else.

CHAPTER FORTY-ONE

A lot happened in the months between the shooting and my arrest.

I lived in a gated community and I was friendly with the security guards at the front entrance. One of the guards told me that two detectives came around asking what kind of car I drove. They wanted a description and the license plate numbers. I was okay with that, but I knew I had to take precautions because I had already seen people with cameras and binoculars following me.

The next day, I left my house and started driving aimlessly around town. I went to a car rental agency and leased a vehicle, leaving my own car in their parking lot. When I went home, I used my clicker to open the gate, but again I drove all around the community before parking my car in a neighbor's driveway. I walked through his backyard to my house and went in through the back door.

The first detective assigned to my case was nice, but he went on vacation and the cop that covered for him was an asshole. I smelled trouble.

As confident as I was that the shooting would be an open and shut case, I took precautions. One of those precautions was to hire the best criminal defense attorney I could find. David Bogenschutz came into my life in a roundabout way.

My dad loved to go to the racetrack. He shared a box with a defense attorney from Coral Gables. When I shot Gurino, I called my father and told him to find me a lawyer. He called his friend from the track, who immediately drove to the precinct in Boca Raton.

When I arrived at the police station, my parents were waiting. The police took a picture of my driver's license and confiscated my phone. There were voice messages on my phone from Gurino from the day before the shooting. The messages were threatening; the police listened to them, but they seemed disinterested. Technology wasn't what it is today. There wasn't any way for them to save the actual messages. The only thing they could do was transcribe them and sign off that they had heard them.

Eventually, a police officer asked if I had a passport, which I didn't. That was it. I wasn't arrested. In fact, the police continued to be very respectful and kind to me. I did not make any statements other than when riding to the precinct with one of the detectives. Trying not to cry, I rambled that I could not take any more threats or face any more danger to myself and my family.

Once I was released from the precinct, I went home. I was emotionally drained and barely able to think. The deli needed to be closed, but I couldn't face going back there. Family members returned to the store to secure it in whatever way they could. The landlord was waiting. He was preparing to have the glass door replaced. In the meantime, he boarded up the entrance with wood. I never stepped a foot in the deli again.

Whenever the newspapers did a story on the shooting, they always referred to me as the innocent victim. Not one reporter doubted that Gurino's had wanted to kill me. I got a job working in a restaurant and felt more at peace than I had in a long time.

Working was a necessity. My wife and I had plenty of bills to pay. We owed a lot on the house that was under construction. As soon as we could, we sold it. Getting our down payment back gave me the money to pay a lawyer. We also sold the house we had been living in and moved into a rental. Every penny was needed to keep our heads above water.

While I wasn't dissatisfied with the attorney my dad had gotten for me, he was based in Miami and was unfamiliar with the Palm Beach County court system. Additionally, there was still the possibility I would be arrested. It's not a good idea to hire an attorney from outside a jurisdiction because he most likely will not have any connections that could help with a case.

David Bogenschutz was a Broward attorney, which also put him on the outside of the Palm Beach County courts. However, he was widely known and well-respected across the state. Based on a recommendation from one of Angelo's friends, someone whom Bogenschutz had represented in a long-ago case, I decided to terminate the first attorney and have Bogenschutz handle my defense should that become needed.

Five or six months passed. The police finally came knocking on my door early on a Sunday morning. I was surprised because I never realized that in the months since Gurino's death, the cops had been trying to build a case against me.

I was barely awake, barefoot and wearing only pajama bottoms. I also had a cast on my hand from a recent surgery and was in significant pain. The police refused to let me get dressed. I was angry. It was embarrassing to be taken from my home at 7:00 am like I was a criminal.

When the police officer leading me out of the house wouldn't give me time to put on a shirt and shoes, I challenged him. "Wait. Let me take off my pajama bottoms. I don't have on any underwear. I might as well be totally naked if you're not going to let me dress decently."

The cop stayed cool. "Mr. Liotta, calm down," he said as he hurried me to a patrol car parked in the driveway. That's when I realized there were news reporters lined up outside with microphones, lights, and cameras at the ready. Someone - the police? - had to have tipped them off. How else would they have known I was going to be arrested?

The little bit of clothing I wore leaving my house was exchanged for a state jumpsuit, which I wore to court the next morning for my arraignment. My mom, dad and wife were in the courtroom. I was embarrassed for them and could see they were nervous for me.

I had no idea what was going on. When I'm nervous, I tend not to hear everything that is said to me. I'm sure when the cops came to my home, they told me what charges had been set against me. I might as well have been deaf. Even in court, I didn't hear the judge, but I'm sure he stated the same charges. The only thing I could hear was my heart pounding in my chest.

As I was sitting and waiting for my case to be called, the door to the courtroom opened and a man I didn't know came in. He was, at least, 50 years old and dressed in a sweater and penny loafers. He gave the impression of being a college professor, and his collegiate style made him seem out of place among the suit and tie crowd.

When my name was called, he got up and stood beside me in front of the judge. I was confused because I was expecting David to represent me. It quickly became obvious that everyone in the courthouse knew this attorney and that he was well respected. I began to relax a bit.

Eventually, I learned that David had hired him so that I could get bail. I believe they had a reciprocal agreement whereby they helped each other with cases out of their normal stomping grounds.

I was released that day, but I still didn't know what charges the prosecutor intended to bring against me. David had been reaching out to the State's Attorney's office, but they were playing their cards close to the chest. At first, he thought they were going to charge me with murder two. He argued for self-defense, but the prosecutor wouldn't budge. For whatever reason, by the time the trial rolled around the prosecutor had changed his mind and charged me with manslaughter.

In the days and months before my arrest, there were things happening that set my nerves on edge, but I never connected them to my case. Several times I saw cops following me and filming me even when I was just having coffee with a friend. Additionally, Gurino's family kept pressuring the newspapers to write a *different* story and, since nobody kills anybody in Boca Raton, the pressure began to get results. I knew I would eventually be arrested; I still didn't believe I would be convicted of a crime.

One of the reasons I felt so confident that a jury would find me innocent was because shortly before Gurino's death a dentist living in a nearby gated community had shot a 14-year-old boy in the back three times. The boy had been terrorizing the neighborhood; knocking on doors and windows and then running away. The dentist was sentenced to weekends in jail for two years.

This case was brought up in court but had little to no effect on the verdict.

CHAPTER FORTY-TWO

By now you might be confused by a life as complicated as mine. I know I've given you a lot of facts and told you a lot of stories, but you might still be wondering how they all fit together in that big jigsaw puzzle I mentioned way back in the beginning of the book.

To be honest, for many years after my conviction for manslaughter in the death of John Gurino, I struggled to make sense of how I could be found guilty of killing someone who was intent on killing me. Most of what I now know, I learned after I was released from prison. It took a while for me to put all the pieces together.

Prison, as I said earlier, is not only boring, it is enforced isolation. You probably think I'm referencing the separation from my wife and son and, while that was a difficult emotional situation to endure, inmates are also isolated from the world at large. For all intents and purposes, prisons are planets floating in a different universe. We have television and books and newspapers, but everything we watch and read is monitored. I didn't know a quarter of what was happening in the on the outside during the 12 years I was inside; not even events that related directly to me and my case.

During my incarceration, my father and brother-in-law clipped hundreds of newspaper articles that mentioned my name, John Gurino or the Gus Boulis case. The stories were all stuffed into big envelopes, awaiting my release. By the time I got home, the pages were turning brown with age. Months passed before I allowed myself to look at them but once I did, I couldn't stop reading. I doubt my lawyer or the prosecutor ever connected the dots with the accuracy shown by some of the self-proclaimed internet crime reporters.

One story, published by David Hopsicker of *Mad Cow Morning News*, offered more information than I could absorb in one reading. I read it for the fifth time while I was preparing to publish this book because each time I look at it, I learn something new.

Hopsicker described his passion as "investigating state sponsored crime." He certainly did that with expert accuracy when it came to Gus Boulis' murder and the eventual death of John Gurino. He was able to unravel an unruly mass of information and reveal the connection between Anthony "Big Tony" Moscatiello, Anthony "Little Tony" Ferrari, James "Pudgy" Fiorello, Adam Kidan and well-known lobbyist Jack Abramoff. Somehow, he was able to create a *family tree* tying together all the players and, since I had killed Gurino, he included me in his story.

According to Hopsicker's article published on May 19, 2007, Adam Kidan (also known as Bagel Boy), a Long Island businessman and associate of Jack Abramoff, admitted to federal investigators that he knew who had murdered Boulis, the founder of Miami Subs and the SunCruz Casino Line. Hopsicker wrote that the details of Boulis' death could implicate high-placed people in the White House – more specifically, the Oval Office – but that would require politicians who really wanted to know the truth, and we all know how important truth is in Washington, D.C.

Kidan's sudden desire to reveal long sought-after facts had nothing to do with a burst of morality or a display of good conscience. He needed neither as the person he identified as the hit man was long dead. Since it is impossible to put a dead man on trial or give him the opportunity to face his accusers in court as the law stipulates, prosecutors had two choices -- take Kidan's word for it or have an open case on their hands until the end of time. They chose the opportunity to boast a win on their record.

In the days immediately following Boulis' death, Kidan was interviewed by the police. He denied having any information about the killing. His denial isn't surprising once you know his background.

Let's start with the "Long Island businessman" moniker. He didn't live on Long Island and he wasn't a businessman, at least, not the average citizen's definition of a businessman.

Adam Kidan went to George Washington University and later graduated from Brooklyn Law School. He campaigned for George H.W. Bush and Ronald Reagan. While still a practicing attorney, he opened two bagel stores in the Hamptons. In the 1990s, he founded a Dial-A-Mattress franchise in Washington, D.C. The White House was one of his clients.

In 2005, Adam Kidan and powerful Republican Party lobbyist Jack Abramoff pleaded guilty to fraud charges in the purchase of the SunCruz Casino Line (2000). Kidan served 27 months in prison and an additional three years on probation. Abramoff was sentenced to six years in federal prison but served only 43 months before being released in 2010.

In 2013, Kidan was a witness for the prosecution in the case against Big Tony Moscatiello, Little Tony Ferrari and Pudgy Fiorello as pertains to the Gus Boulis murder trial. This is when he shook his Magic 8 Ball and my name floated to the surface.

Shortly before the Gus Boulis' slaying, Kidan wrote checks totaling more than $200,000 to Moscatiello, Ferrari and Fiorello. He told investigators that the information he had on Boulis' murder was received from Big Tony. He claimed, however, that Moscatiello never told him the name of the shooter. Pointing the finger at John Gurino was an assumption he made on his own after reading that Gurino had died during a confrontation with a deli owner in Boca Raton, Florida. That deli owner would be me.

Here's an interesting tidbit. By the time Kidan made his Magic 8 Ball revelation to the authorities, I was three years into my sentence. Because of statements he made, I was called to testify in the case the state brought against Moscatiello, Ferrari and Fiorello. My sole purpose was to paint a picture of Gurino as a brutal killer based on my experience with him. Speaking the truth had never been easier.

As is standard procedure, witnesses are not allowed in the courtroom during proceedings until they are called to give testimony. I spent my waiting time sitting on a bench in the hallway. Another man was waiting as well. I didn't know him, and we did not acknowledge each other.

The man kept himself busy talking on the telephone. It wasn't until the bailiff came out of the courtroom that I learned his identity. "Mr. Kidan, it will just be a few more minutes."

At the mention of the man's name, my head turned quickly in his direction. "You're Kidan?"

He looked at me warily. "Yeah. Why?"

"I'm Liotta."

The blood drained from his face. "You're not mad at me, are you, for telling them about Gurino?"

I laughed. "Mad at you. No. I'm grateful. You got three years taken off my sentence."

That was the extent of our conversation, but I could see the color coming back into his face as he took a deep, relaxing breath.

CHAPTER FORTY-THREE

Shooting described as revenge slaying
Palm Beach Post

Boca deli manager shoots associate
Palm Beach Post

Suspected mob member gunned down
United Press International (UPI)

Shooting at deli was in self-defense, deputies say
Sun Sentinel

Shooting is labeled self-defense
Sun Sentinel

Deli manager charged in Gotti backer's death
Associated Press

Man charged in deli slaying released on $50,000 bond
Palm Beach Post

BREAD AND BULLETS

Deli owner's manslaughter trial opens
Sun Sentinel

Mob's reach is on view in Florida murder trial
New York Times

Ex-deli owner found guilty of manslaughter
Palm Beach Post

Deli owner gets 15 years in jail
Sun Sentinel

Deli owner who shot suspected mob hit man to remain in jail
Sun Sentinel

When a crime involves a member of the mob or, in my case, someone the prosecution is determined to label a member of the mob, the defendant is convicted in the headlines before the presiding judge bangs his gavel against the sound block to open the trial. I could fill the next 20 pages of this book with stories that, at first, painted me as an innocent victim and, later, a cold-blooded killer. Innocent victim isn't news worthy. Cold-blooded killer? That's manna from heaven to investigative reporters.

There was only one reason why I shot John Gurino, and it had nothing to do with revenge or greed as some headlines proclaimed. Only one reason. Fear.

I believed that when he reached into his pocket, he was reaching for the gun I had seen earlier in the day. Shooting him was instinctual. I wanted to live. He wanted me dead.

My trial began on January 24, 2005. I was confident that my plea of self-defense would rule the day, and I would walk out of court a free man. David Bogenschutz, my attorney, was equally sure that the jury would see that my options were limited to two – shoot or be shot.

In mid-April 2018, my wife was watching an episode of the TV series, *Bull*. The main character, Jason Bull, a trial psychologist, made a statement about people who think they can determine how a jury will vote before the verdict is announced.

It went something like this, "If anyone tells you they know how a criminal proceeding is going to end, they have never been to more than one."

When I heard those words, I was immediately brought back to the opening day of my trial. David was positive that the jury would find me not guilty. Because of his confidence in both his ability to make the jury see the truth and the absolute facts of the case, I, too, believed I would be found not guilty. Imagine our surprise when those six men and women thumbed their noses at us.

Abraham Lincoln said, "He who represents himself has a fool for a client." I'd like to paraphrase that a bit and state, "A defendant who thinks with absolute certainty that he can read a jury's mind is himself a fool."

On day one of the trial, David and I were riding high, confident that my innocent verdict was in the bag. There were six people on the jury, and they all seemed intelligent and interested in hearing the facts. On day two, Assistant State's Attorney Bunnie Lenhardt came to us with the tentative offer of a plea deal – three years in prison. I could have done three years wearing the same pair of underwear, but David countered with "No prison time." That was the last we heard from her.

Day three brought a chill to the air. We sensed a change in the jury. Prosecutor Lenhardt was doing a good job of turning them against me. By mid-afternoon, David and I felt like two of the men left behind on the Titanic, listening as the band played *Nearer My God to Thee*.

At 5 pm on Friday afternoon (Day 5), the jury foreman asked Judge Rapp for the transcripts relating to the medical examiner's report. The judge informed him that the information requested would not be available until Monday. He instructed the foreman to return to the jury and encourage them to reach a verdict.

I should point out here that the "suggestion" by the judge went against what the jury had been told by the Prosecutor during closing arguments. "I might misstate something that you heard. By all means, take your own collective memory. And if there's still any question, there's always other avenues if you need to, okay?"

Obviously, the jury did have questions, but they did not bother to pursue those other avenues Prosecutor Lenhardt mentioned in great part due to Judge Rapp's advice. They reached a verdict a short time later. Their few hours of deliberation resulted in a 15-year prison sentence.

While one thing or many things could have swayed the jury to cast a guilty verdict, I believe it was the report by the medical examiner and testimony by Deputy Eric Keith, which the jury heard during the trial, that was most injurious.

Medical Examiners report (as per the Probable Cause Affidavit/Deputy Eric Keith 12/22/2003):

"Dr. Lisa Flannagan, Chief Medical Examiner, conducted an on-scene investigation and performed an autopsy of (John) Gurino's remains on October 29, 2003. She determined the cause of death to be multiple gunshot wounds and the manner of death to be homicide. Gurino suffered four gunshot wounds. There was no indication of stippling or contact wounds. One gunshot wound was into the right side of Gurino's chest; the projectile traveled from right to left, upward and slightly from front to back, through Gurino's chest and lodged in Gurino's left upper arm (after breaking the bone). Another gunshot wound was in Gurino's right lower back. The wound track passed from back to front, slightly upward, and right to left. A third bullet wound was in Gurino's right lateral buttock. The wound track passed from right to left and slightly upward. Dr. Flannagan found a final gunshot wound in Gurino's right upper buttock. The wound traveled from back to front, upward, and right to left. There were no identified gunshot wounds with front to rear wound tracks. All gunshots were fired at Gurino from the side or from behind."

In his statement, Deputy Eric Keith said that Dr. Flannagan and a crime scene investigator had "found an unsheathed knife with about a three-inch blade completely inside Gurino's front right pants pocket." He further stated, "The knife was not visible until the contents of the pocket were emptied. There were seven empty shell casings found inside the store (Corner Deli) near the entrance."

It was Deputy Keith's opinion that "Given Gurino's final resting position, Liotta's position at the time the shots were fired and the position of the shell casings, there was room for retreat deeper into the business or behind the front counter. It should be noted that the crime scene investigator found a loaded .38 caliber revolver inside Gurino's truck."

As I said earlier in this book, had the *Stand Your Ground Law* been in effect at the time of the shooting, I would never have seen the inside of a courtroom. Why? The shooting of John Gurino is a text book example of the Law's definition in action.

In a criminal case where the *Stand Your Ground Law* is applied, defendants have the right to stand and fight back when faced with actual or perceived threats. Furthermore, defendants have "no duty to retreat" from a place they lawfully have the right to occupy, such as my store. According to the law, defendants may use any level of force believed necessary when faced with the threat of bodily harm or death. That's exactly what I did.

For Deputy Keith, a man who has most likely faced death on occasion in his profession as a law enforcement officer, to state that I could have "retreated deeper into the business" is unconscionable. There was no back door... no other way out. Had I retreated and Gurino followed me, as I anticipated he would do, I would have been trapped. Since I had seen a gun in his waistband and he had made no secret of his desire to kill me, I did what any person in my position would have done.

Florida's Stand Your Ground Law went into effect on October 1,

2005, less than eight months after my guilty verdict was delivered by the jury.

Trials, even murder trials, are often tedious and boring. Jurors are people whose lives have been put on hold while they do their civic duty. Many, if not most, of them don't want to serve, but they are bound by law to pretend they care what happens to a stranger whose actions have inconvenienced them. The thought of spending another minute confined to an airless room was all the incentive those six men and women needed to reach an agreement.

People who have never been subjected to a criminal proceeding are always interested in the plea deal. Everyone wants to know why I didn't insist that David pursue the offer… why I didn't insist that he negotiate a deal. If you are a first-time offender, you have no idea what you can or cannot do… what you should or shouldn't do. I would never refer to myself as naïve, but I was a babe in the woods during the trial.

In a criminal case, the cast of characters resembles a Superman comic book. The defendant is always portrayed as bad and the prosecutor as the champion of truth, justice and the American way. The defense attorney… he's also bad… someone who would sell his own mother if the price was high enough. A trial pits good versus evil, with the scales leaning heavily toward the prosecution even before the facts are known.

Defendants don't have much to say during their trial. They are not only mute with despair; they are lost spiritually, mentally and emotionally, burdened by the knowledge that the right to live the rest of their life as they choose is dependent on the mercy of other people. They cannot jump tall buildings in a single bound; they can't even walk freely, shackled as they are by the lies presented as facts.

The six jurors and one alternate in my case were incapable of empathy. They saw a wealthy man wearing expensive clothing, driving an expensive car... a man who had a beautiful young wife and many, many friends in the courtroom who also were monied.

They were afraid of me. I wasn't like them. I didn't look like them and, unfortunately, I talked like the mobsters portrayed in every Hollywood movie ever produced. They saw me as someone who had never known what it was like to struggle. I was someone who had never worried about paying the rent or putting food on the table. I lived well. I was everything they weren't and, maybe, wished they could be.

Forced to choose between a longer deliberation and going home, they just wanted to go home at the end of the day. I don't fault them. I'm not angry with them. They didn't know me.

Thanks to television and the movies, jurors view prosecutors as the good guys and defense attorneys as the devil in a three-piece suit. They did their best with the information that was given to them and their limited knowledge of violence and victimization.

CHAPTER FORTY-FOUR

When the guilty verdict was announced, everyone in my family began crying. Not me. What good would crying do. Plus, it would only upset my wife and parents more to see me break down. I gave my dad my phone and personal effects, and the guards led me out of the courtroom. I was taken to a room on the first floor where I signed a form agreeing to my guilty verdict. Once you sign that form, you become the property of the state.

From the courthouse, I was returned to the county jail in West Palm Beach. I had no idea what to expect. Anyone who came near me, I plied with questions. Both other inmates and guards assured me that prison would be better than jail... more options, more space, a chance to work. I got the impression that prison was one big schoolyard.

So, I waited... and waited and waited for someone to come and get me. Doors opened and were banged shut. Other prisoners left, but I was still sitting in a cell... waiting for the unknown to become known.

The next stop in my journey through the Florida prison system was the intake center in Miami. It's a terrible place. Just hope that you never have to go there. If you do, it will be like entering hell while still alive.

The move took place at 2:30 am with an unceremonious wake up call. Five buses were parked outside the jail. By the time the buses were loaded and ready to pull out of the parking lot, it was almost 4 am. There were 40 to 60 inmates on each bus and all of us were shackled. Each bus had only one bathroom. It was a two-hour drive to Miami. There was a thick fog, which made it impossible to see out the windows. Alfred Hitchcock could not have written this scene any better.

The sun was up when we reached the intake center. Looking through the window, all I could see were barbed wire fences and gun towers. The gate opened, and the first two buses passed through. I was on the third bus. Time passed. The gate opened again. Once inside, the bus was inspected with mirrors on long poles, looking for escapees and contraband.

After entering the intake center, we were broken up in groups. Twenty men at a time were told to stand in a circle and strip naked. While completely nude, we were sprayed with a chemical powder meant for de-licing. The spray covered us everywhere, including our hair and private parts. It burned and caused welts to form. The longer it stuck to your skin, the more intense the burning became.

We were finally marched into a shower with spigots sticking out of the wall. The water was hot and burned even worse than the chemical on our skin. It didn't matter. We just wanted to wash the powder away by whatever means possible.

After washing, we were given black shower slippers and red shorts to wear. Our heads were shaved. Each inmate was given a brown bag, which was placed on the floor at their feet. We were told not to touch the bag. Inside was a tooth brush and tooth paste. We were also given three pairs of underwear, three pairs of socks and three tee shirts. The underwear had already been worn by previous inmates. You could tell. Trust me.

I was offended by the condition of the underwear and couldn't stop myself from complaining. The officer in charge told me all the underwear had previously been worn, but he allowed me to look for a pair in better condition. I wore that pair until I had access to my inmate's bank account. Then, I bought clean underwear from the laundry room attendant.

There came a point when we were told to put our personal effects in the bag. I saw another guy put his glasses in, so I did the same. A Corrections Officer jumped up and smashed me into a chain link fence. "You touched the bag," he screamed. I pointed to my glasses.

The CO was furious and marched me into another room where I was made to stand facing a wall for 90 minutes. He said he was going to lock me in the box for 60 days.

I guess I was supposed to be scared, but I said, "Wow. You're a big, tough guy."

He got angrier. "I'm a tough guy? You've had it. You've had it."

"Go ahead. Push me into the fence again so I can sue your ass."

That CO left, and another replaced him. This guy was nicer. He did whatever needed to be done to get me out of there. I was taken back to the front desk where the first guy was sitting. Among my personal items were pictures of my wife and son. I always slept with them next to my chest for comfort and so no one would steal them.

The CO who harassed me said, "You ain't taking these things with you," and he crumbled them up. He stared at me, "What do you think of that?"

I stared back but I said nothing.

Into another room we went, where we again had to wait. Ten minutes passed. A CO entered the room, yelling my name. He gave me my photos and told me that someone had taken them out of the trash. I never found out who it was.

The intake center was built in the shape of a "T" with the top of the "T" being shorter than the rest of the building. The dorms were to the right and the left. There were two floors of dorms with two showers in each dorm. Each of the dorms had a name based on a letter of the alphabet. I was in "L" for Lima.

Lima dorm was built in the 1960s. It was old. Each inmate was given a bed liner, blanket, sheet and pillow case, which he had to put on his head and carry to his assigned spot. By the time all the requirements for intake had been met, we were dead tired and starving. There had been no breakfast, and lunchtime was nearly over. We were allowed five minutes to eat whatever food was available. The process was the same every day... five minutes to eat and out. I was a slow eater. There were a lot of days I never got to finish my meals.

The showers in the dorms were filthy with standing water that reached past our ankles. There was no shampoo and only lye soap with which to wash. After a few days, I found garbage bags to tie around my feet, so I didn't pick up any diseases.

The bars of soap were small and didn't last long. If you ran out, you had to knock on the officer's window and request another bar. There was a sign on the window: *If you're white, don't knock.* No kidding. When I needed soap, I had to ask an inmate of color to get it for me.

Outside became the go to place. After breakfast... after lunch... we were always forced to stand in the hot sun. Because most of the prisoners had never been bald, their heads burned and blistered. The blisters filled with pus. It was not uncommon to be talking with another inmate and have one of those blisters burst and spew pus on everyone and everything. Disgusting!

The second day at the intake center was spent getting medical and dental checkups. The dental office had six chairs. Teeth were x-rayed and documented. I can still see the face of one of the guys in my dorm. He spent an unusually long time with the dentist (four hours) and when he returned, he was swollen and in obvious pain. I asked him what happened. He told me he had eight teeth pulled. I was shocked, but he felt it was the only way he would ever get new dentures. For him, prison represented health insurance.

A lot of screaming goes on at the intake center... mostly it's the Corrections Officers yelling at the inmates. The morning we arrived, a CO got on the bus and set the tone for the remainder of our stay. "All right, motherfuckers. My wife's cheating on me with my neighbor. I can't freaking believe it. I'm gonna take it out on you."

He grabbed one of the prisoners by the neck and continued to scream in his face. The other inmates were getting scared. Not me.

Intimidation has never been an effective means of getting me to do anything.

Since incarceration at the intake center is temporary – it's a weigh station... the final checkpoint before assignment to a permanent prison... cells and cell mates change often. Sometimes, if I was lucky, I was confined to a tiny cell (5' x 8') that had twin bunk beds and a toilet. Sometimes, I was alone. Other times, not. I always tried to get the top bunk because the rats were less likely to climb so high. The room was hot... very hot. It had a window that was covered with a perforated steel plate, but the holes did not provide any ventilation.

Experienced guys – those who had been in prison more than once - had a system for staying cool. They rigged plastic bags and pieces of cardboard over the holes in the window, creating a tunnel. The tunnel directed whatever breeze there might be toward the bunks.

There was a short period when I bunked with a guy who had been in prison seven times. My parents had given me money, so I was able to buy decent food, like cheeseburgers and Cokes. My cellmate was a chain smoker, but he didn't have any money to buy cigarettes. Sometimes, just to be nice, I bought them for him.

One particularly hot day, I bought a writing pad at the canteen. Since I'm dyslexic and a poor speller, I never wrote to anyone. I used the pad to fan myself.

My cellmate, who went through cigs like they were candy, began asking me every day to buy him another pack. In desperation, he made me an offer I couldn't refuse... buy him smokes and he would fan me to sleep. We had a deal.

If I got up to go to the bathroom, he would fan me until I fell back to sleep. Prison makes men do the unthinkable.

The two weeks I spent at the intake center felt like an eternity. Prison was starting to look good to me.

CHAPTER FORTY-FIVE

I was among the first groups of inmates to be housed at South Bay. The facility was new and consisted of two buildings. Each building had two floors of five pods each. Sixty-four men were housed in each pod. My pod had only five inmates to start, but it filled up by the end of the week.

At check in, we were each given a new mattress. We had to carry it to our rooms, but it was no big deal. The doors to the rooms had buttons which the inmates used to let themselves in and out. Three times a day, a count was taken. During these times, all the doors were locked. They were also locked at night. Truthfully, it wasn't much different than a hotel.

South Bay Correctional Facility - a private state prison. Private is code for *you pay for everything*.

Once I was processed into South Bay, I was given a photocopy of the *Inmate Handbook*. A quick look at the table of contents, and I felt an imaginary hand smack me in the back of the head. Prison? What prison? I was going to summer camp.

South Bay offered academic, vocational, substance abuse and institutional betterment programs (Alcoholics and Narcotics Anonymous).

There was a library and recreational activities were provided. Recreation was touted as a means of keeping prisoners in good physical condition, but it was really meant to keep them busy and out of trouble.

Delving deeper into the *Inmate Handbook*, I learned there were Education, Library, and Chaplaincy Services available. The second page listed Laundry Services, Mail, Telephones, Food Service, and Medical and Dental. Also, on the second page was a listing for Inmate Banking – Subheading: How to Send Money. I quickly flipped to page 27 because I had no idea why I would need to send or receive money in prison. Before the day was over, I would know all I needed to know, and it was an eye opener. The summer camp illusion quickly dissolved.

"Money talks" is a popular expression, but nowhere does it speak louder than in prison. Inmates need money if they want to maintain even a modicum of normalcy. While prison is a cash-less facility, each prisoner does have an account into which family members can make deposits and from which the prisoner can make withdrawals. Money can be used to buy personal items from the canteen (store) and a better-quality food than is provided by the system. The money is also used to pay for any outside services an inmate might need, such as legal supplies (pen, paper, legal forms, photocopying and typing services, etc.) which help facilitate the appeal or retrial process. If an inmate wants clean clothes, i.e. underwear without skid marks, he must pay one of the laundry room attendants for that service. As I said, "money talks" and in prison, talking comes with lots of dollar signs.

The first time I turned in my laundry at South Bay, it included three pairs of new "blue" pants. "Blues" are what we called the standard uniform. When my laundry was returned, there were only two pairs of pants. Nobody knew where the other pair had gone.

Later in the day, I was sitting in the canteen eating when a guy walked by wearing new pants. The name on the pocket was crossed out but I could still read "L I O T." I grabbed the back of his shirt and pulled. He yelled, "Man, you don't touch me!"

I said, "You're wearing my pants. Take them off." The bickering began.

"I told you don't touch me."

"Take off my pants."

The guy lowered his face to mine, and I head butted him... smashed his nose. He fell to the ground, stunned. I had a big lump on my forehead. I finished eating while waiting for him to return to his room. Then, I followed. When he saw me, he took off my pants and shrugged as he gave them back to me. "I got 12 pairs of stolen pants. I don't need yours."

The next day, I bought new blues – the ones with a stripe down the leg. I kept these to wear on visitor's day, so my family would never know how bad it was inside.

Five or six years into my sentence, I requested a transfer to the Martin County Prison System. Martin County is a level six prison – the worst of the worst. Often called the Alcatraz of Florida, the buildings are old and in desperate need of repair. There was lots of gang activity. Rats outnumbered prisoners and had free run of the facility. Despite all the reasons not to want to be an inmate in Martin County, there was one very good reason for going there. It was the only way to get into the work release program.

Work camp is as close as an inmate can get to the outside world. While the physical labor is hard, it is worth every drop of sweat that drips from our pores. Work camp and work release offer hope... hope was in short supply among the general population crowd.

Work camp is usually granted to inmates who have 36 or fewer months left on their sentence. They must have maintained a trouble-free existence while incarcerated. Inmates sentenced for a sexual offense or with a history of sexual offenses are not eligible for the program.

While on work release, prisoners live in a community correctional center and maintain full-time employment. A portion of their salary is used to pay for their room and board and a portion is put into a mandatory savings account. Disciplinary action of any kind will quickly send an inmate back to prison.

When I left South Bay, I wasn't allowed to take any of my personal belongings – things like peanut butter, jelly and Tupperware containers. Remember, I said we had to buy our food? These items were a necessary part of our meal plans. Didn't matter. They all got dumped in a box.

There was another inmate who was moving to Martin County at the same time I did. He had no idea what he could keep and what he had to throw away. In his confusion, he tossed three pairs of underwear only to realize he should have kept them. When he ran back to retrieve them, the guards tackled him and gave him a beating. Inmates have a target on their backs, and they never know who is taking aim.

At South Bay, there were two rooms where inmates met their visitors. One room had vending machines and microwave ovens along a long wall. On one side of the room was the toilet for inmates. Along the wall with the vending machines was a bathroom for visitors.

Remember, inmates go without intimacy for years. Some of the guys were jonesing for a little TLC. They were clever. When they had a female visitor, they would work together so that they could each have a little private time with their wife or girlfriend.

There was a system. The inmates would line up one behind the other along the wall with the vending machines. They would leave enough space for a visitor to walk between them and the machines without being seen. The wife or girlfriend would go into the bathroom, and the inmate would follow. They would have their time together and then leave.

I understood why many of the men participated in this farce, but I could never bring myself to do that to Sheryl. I was in prison for years, but I never once asked her to dishonor herself in that way. It was wrong. Everyone knew what was going on. The women would come out looking disheveled. It was embarrassing.

During one visit, I could see that Sheryl was upset. She had Rosario, Jr. and my son Jimmy and his girlfriend with her. I kept asking her what was wrong, but she wouldn't tell me.

Picture this... visitors are forced to wait on line outside the prison in all kinds of weather. They can be out there in the broiling sun or pouring rain for as long as three hours.

There were 2400 inmates and only two visiting days. Each visiting day, 1200 inmates got to spend a few hours with their loved ones. It took time to move people in and out of the prison, but no accommodations were made for family and friends.

I am the type of person who, when I know there is a problem, I want to find a solution. I never know when to stop asking questions, so seeing that Sheryl was upset, I kept at her until she finally told me what was wrong.

While she and the kids were waiting to be let into the prison, another visitor – a tall, older man - started putting the moves on her. He pretended they had already met. Told Sheryl some nonsense about being a pilot and taking people skiing in Vail.

I was furious. Sheryl is beautiful. I'm used to men looking at her, but this was different. Coming to visit anyone in prison is traumatic. She had the kids with her... she didn't know what to expect when she got inside. She was vulnerable.

During the visit, the kids got hungry. I went to the vending machines and got sandwiches. I saw the man Sheryl had described with a younger guy – obviously, his son - who was an inmate. Sheryl got up to go to the bathroom, and the guy stopped her... tried talking to her again. I put the sandwiches down and confronted him.

"If you say one more word to my wife, I'm going to beat the shit out of you."

I berated him for taking advantage of women who were already traumatized by coming to the prison. I told him if I ever saw him talking to my wife again, I would beat his son, and his son would never know when I was coming to get him. I was yelling so loud; the guard rushed over.

I told him what had happened and, being a little sympathetic, he told me to calm down. The guard took Sheryl aside. She told him the whole story. From then on, our visiting days were switched. I don't remember ever seeing the son after that day either.

Imagine, these poor women, some of them with kids, are scared and lonely and some jerk dangles a plane ride and trip to Vail. That guy was a predator.

CHAPTER FORTY-SIX

Teaching judo kept me out of trouble at South Bay. I took judo as a kid, so I knew what I was doing. There was already a guy working with the inmates, but he would hurt them intentionally. When I took over the class, we did floor exercise and submission moves. I made pads in upholstery class, so the guys would have protection. When I wasn't doing that I would run, use the weight room or paint... anything to keep my mind occupied.

Believe it or not, I was also a motivational speaker. I didn't really like it, so I would always find a way to focus the spotlight on someone else. The way I would do that... I would start to tell a story and, without fail, someone would say, "Yeah, but I heard it differently." This was my chance to say, "Come on up here and share your story." Then, I would sit down and let him run the class.

I had a favorite story I liked to tell the other inmates. "There was a kid, a teenager, who lived at home with his parents. Because he was dyslexic, like me, he could never get a good job. His parents were getting fed up with him. His father gave him an ultimatum, "Get a job or find somewhere else to live."

The father wasn't being cruel. He was trying to incentivize his son.

A friend of the family owned a hardware store in the neighborhood and was looking for a helper. The dad told his son to apply for the job.

The kid got hired, but part of his responsibilities was to log the chemicals on a spreadsheet. Since he couldn't write, he couldn't do his job, and the friend had to fire him. The kid was embarrassed, and the father felt sorry for him.

He said to his son, "Listen, when your brother moved away, he left his dump truck in the backyard. It needs work… tires, oil, brakes… go get it fixed. I'll pay for it, and you can pay me back when you earn some money. Go to all the construction sites and see if you can pick up some odd jobs.

The kid was excited. He started small, moving wood and dirt. The business grew. He hired one helper and then another. After six months, he bought another truck and paid his dad back the money he had been loaned. Before he knew it, he owned eight trucks and business was booming. In a few years, he was a multi-millionaire.

He decided to surprise his parents by buying them a new house. He found just the right place, hired a lawyer and, without telling his parents why, he brought them to the attorney's office, so they could sign the ownership papers. The parents protested, but the son insisted.

The lawyer slid a legal document across to the kid and told him to sign it. He puts an X on the paper. The lawyer said, "You've got to sign your name."

Embarrassed, the kid said, "I can't write." The lawyer was shocked. Here was a kid worth more than $12 million, but he couldn't read or write. The lawyer collected his thoughts and said," Just imagine where you would be if you had gone to school and gotten an education."

The kid responded, "Yeah. You know where I would be? I'd be a stock boy down at the hardware store."

The guys always loved that story. I would tell them that no matter what job they undertook, they should do it the best way they knew how. Every day, they needed to do the job the same way, but every day, they needed to go one step further. Little steps, not giant leaps. I told them not to try to do more than they knew how to do. Just take it slow and learn something new every day.

I can't spell, but I can read... mostly because I know what certain words look like. I guess that's called sight reading. When I was at South Bay, I used the ability to "see" solutions to help inmates learn math. Everyone was given a math book with algebra and geometry problems. All the answers were in the back of the book. I would look at the problems and then look at the answers. Once I saw the answer, I would turn the problem around in my head, working my way backwards to the problem. That's how I taught the other guys.

I did make friends with one guy while I was in prison. He was an old Italian guy. He overheard me talking to my family in the visitor's room and asked, "Are you Italian?"

I said "Yeah," and we started talking. He was a nice guy, even introduced me to his family. It turned out we had met years before when I was into the club scene. The old guy and I start hanging out together. Some inmates told me he was a rat, and I should watch out for him. I didn't listen. I treat everybody nice until they do something that proves I shouldn't.

The longer I knew this man, the more I realized what it was the other guys didn't like about him. He wasn't a rat. He was a nosy body. He never stopped asking questions. If you answered his first question, he asked a hundred more. I finally told him he had to "Shut up" or the guys were going to beat his ass. During our friendship, I pulled so many practical jokes on him, he wanted to kill me, but he couldn't because he was laughing too hard. He was a good guy.

Mostly, I just stayed alone.

CHAPTER FORTY-SEVEN

The Colonel who oversaw work release was a nice guy. I got to know him while I was at the work camp in Martin County. In fact, he was the reason I was on work release in West Palm Beach.

During his many visits to the work camp, I would help him load gasoline and supplies for his compound in Palm Beach County. He was friendly, and we talked a lot. The Colonel, understanding that work camp was the first step in the release process, asked me if I had been thinking ahead. I told him I was hoping for work release in West Palm Beach, as it would bring me closer to home. He made that happen.

Not long after that conversation, as I was getting ready to go to work camp, a guard told me to "… pack it up." I was surprised and merely stared at him. He said, "Come on. You're going to work release." The smile that spread across my face was huge. I was happy and wanted to take nothing with me that would remind me of my time in work camp. Everything I owned, I gave to the other guys. I put my personal belongings… toothbrush, tooth paste, hairbrush… in a small paper bag and ran for the door.

Outside a van was waiting. Three other men were already inside, We were taken to the work release center. It's protocol for inmates on work release to take classes before they are sent out to find a job. Most guys don't have any prospects, so it's harder for them. Often, months pass before they find employment. Remember, I worked in the tool room in prison, so maintenance seemed like a good fit.

When I arrived at work release, I already had a job lined up, but I never told anyone. The man who had been my maintenance supervisor in Martin County had been reassigned to West Palm Beach, and he asked me to paint the women's dorms. He knew I was capable, and I guess he thought he was doing me a favor. Basically, I had a job from day one, but it was a job I didn't want.

Painting the dorms was going to take time and would delay my ability to work outside the compound. I told the supervisor and he understood. He took my paperwork and had it approved. My reputation as a standup guy during all the years I was incarcerated worked in my favor.

Being on work release is as close to freedom as an inmate is ever going to get. You live in a compound which resembles a motel. The compound where I was assigned was located at the Fairgrounds in West Palm Beach. Usually, three prisoners share a room and two rooms share a bathroom. The setup isn't ideal, but it's a lot better than a jail cell.

If you have money, you can live well on these programs. While at work camp, I was able to buy a good mattress and clean sheets. I also got the bed directly under the fan. Without the mattress and the fan, sleeping would have been impossible. Comfort is not a priority where inmates are concerned.

Not everyone on work release has the same values. Since the men could now have a cell phone, talking all night long became an issue. Phones would ring at all hours only they weren't just ringing. They were playing rap songs at ridiculous decibels.

I had a roommate, a young kid, who had no consideration for the long hours I worked or for anyone else trying to keep a job. His phone was constantly waking us up. After a few "discussions" on courtesy and his refusal to listen, I threw him out into the courtyard and locked the door. He screamed and pounded on the door until the guards came and took us both to the office.

I knew most of the security people from my years in the main prison. I asked one of them to call the Colonel and tell him what had happened. The Colonel said, "Are you out of your minds. This man is working his ass off. He's making good money for himself and for the system. Send him back to his room and let him sleep, and if he needs a room to himself, find one. Send the other guy back."

I didn't want any special favors and I didn't want the kid to go back to prison. We talked, came to an agreement, and we both went back to the room. Now, he tries to *friend* me on Facebook.

The reason I already had a job waiting when I got to work release was that I'm the kind of person who anticipates what the future might hold. Even though I'm not formally educated, and I don't know how everything works, I have always had the ability to think outside the box. For example, when I was in prison, I realized that my driver's license was about to expire, and I would have no way of reinstating it. I asked my daughter to file a change of address with motor vehicle, making my parents' house my legal residence. I knew that by doing that, the expiration date of my license would be extended. It wasn't that I needed to drive while incarcerated. I just wanted to keep the license active because, in some strange way, it made me feel like I still had an identity beyond my Department of Corrections number. As it happened, my license did expire two weeks before I was released, but it wasn't a big problem to get it renewed.

Just as with my driver's license, when work release began to look like a reality, I called Gio and asked for a job. He was more than happy to help me. The market was in Palm Beach County but it was out of the jurisdiction covered by the work release program. My being there required special permission. Again, the Colonel took care of that.

Prisoners need the proper clothing to go to work. Most don't have money to buy new jeans or even a jacket for the cold weather. My parents had to buy me pants and shirts. Prisoners do not have cars, nor are they allowed to take a cab. Families can buy a bicycle and a cell phone for an inmate to make getting a job easier. Most travel by bus. I had never taken a bus in my life. I didn't know where the bus stops were located or how to pay.

The first day I left the compound for work would make a great comedy routine. I stood at a bus stop with some of the other guys, and they tried to explain to me how the routes worked. They gave me directions… "Take the next bus to the third stop. Then, take bus #224 to Whatever Street. Wait for bus #36 and take it to the last stop." My head was spinning. They even had to tell me to pull the cord, so the driver would know I wanted to get off. I felt stupid, but I wanted to do everything right, so I learned quickly.

When I reached my last stop on that first day, I got a big surprise. My whole family was waiting on the street corner. They had gotten up early and gone together to the market so that I wouldn't be alone. It was one of the best days of my life.

After a week of taking the bus, Gio took pity on me. He and his family hired a driver to pick me up every morning and bring me back to camp at night. The Colonel allowed it because it didn't financially impact his budget and made it easier for me to work longer hours. One day, the driver came in a Maserati. It was raining, and he got out of the car with an umbrella, so I wouldn't get wet. I told him, "No way you are to come back here in this car and do not hold an umbrella for me. You're not my servant." Can you imagine what the other guys must have thought?

CHAPTER FORTY-EIGHT

Under the best of circumstances, it can be difficult living with people. Now, imagine what it's like living with thousands of people you've never met before and have no interest in knowing. Add to that situation the loss of privacy and the threat of punishment for infractions big and small. Prison is like being married without any of the benefits and every one of the drawbacks.

People come and go... cellmates change without any warning. Sometimes they stay for a few weeks or months, other times they disappear overnight. Adjustments and compromises must constantly be made, but not everyone is willing to do that. No two people are alike. Different cultures. Different beliefs. Different routines. Annoying habits. Who picks their nose. Who picks their toes. Who scratches or tosses and turns all night long. There is no escape. You're stuck in a small room with nowhere to go. During count times, to sleep, to use the toilet... togetherness is forced upon you. It's almost impossible to form a bond and, probably, better if you don't.

There was a young black kid who was brought to South Bay while I was there. He was a bag of bones... skinny... and he had a bad limp. He was also from New York which gave us something in common. We would talk, and for a few weeks things were good. I could tell he was a trouble maker, but he seemed to save the worst of his temperament for when he was in general population.

We had a few problems... smoking for one. I don't smoke. He smoked weed all day and night, even in the wee hours of the morning. I would ask him to stop, and he would snap at me. Weed made his bad temper worse.

When he first arrived, he told me that he had been in a different dorm where he roomed with a friend. The friend had him thrown out because he snored so badly. No matter how much he pleaded, the friend wouldn't let him back in the cell. That's how he came to be my cellmate.

Snoring is a big issue in prison, but it can be easily resolved. All an inmate needs is a pair of ear plugs. Unfortunately, some inmates refuse to use them. Hence, the constant need to play musical cells.

The skinny kid roomed with me in the winter. I got the flu; I was terribly sick. There were two lockers in our cell, one for each of us. Because I was so congested, I started snoring – loud. The kid began pounding on the lockers. Boom! Boom! Boom! I jumped out of bed. "What? Are you nuts? Don't go banging on the lockers."

He accused me of snoring intentionally so that he would get kicked out of the room. I called him a few names and warned him again not to bang on the lockers. I fell back to sleep. As soon as I started snoring, he was back to banging on the lockers. This time when I jumped out of bed, I grabbed him by the throat. He yelled at the top of his lungs.

A female corrections officer rushed into the dorm and told me to let him go. She unlocked the cell and pushed the kid out into the hallway. He was still screaming. I told the CO what happened. She decided to take us to the control room.

The control room was where all the officers spent their time. Prisoners tried to avoid going there because they wanted to keep a low profile. It cramped their style if the guards could see them all the time.

The walk to the control room took us down some long corridors inside and outside the building. The kid and I were both handcuffed. The female CO walked us in, and the kid immediately started accusing me of being prejudiced. He was playing to one of the black officers.

The officer asked us both for our inmate numbers. He used them to search for our records in the computer. We were standing directly in front of him as he typed. After a while, he looked at us and asked, "Not for nothing, but Liotta has been here for four years and doesn't have one complaint against him. You've been here less than six months, and you've been in trouble three times. Who am I going to believe?'

The kid started yelling again, and the officer held up his hand. "That's it. Liotta, you go back to your dorm. You (talking to the kid), you're staying in this building."

The kid freaked. "I don't want to stay here."

We were both sent outside to wait for an escort. The kid started pleading with me to drop the complaint and let him come back to our room. I told him I wouldn't take any more of his crap, but I'd give him a second chance. I went back into the office and told the CO that the kid could stay in the cell with me. The CO made me sign a release stating that my life wasn't in danger. Then, he said, "Go. Go back to the dorm. I don't want any more trouble from either of you."

We started walking to our dorm along the perimeter fence back. We were alone. No guards. The kid was a little ahead of me. We were barely out of earshot of the control room when he started in again. "Liotta, good thing you did that, motherfucker. I would've gotten you otherwise. I would get you, man."

I walked up behind him and hit him hard in the back of the head. His face met the ground and stayed there. I kept walking. When I got to my dorm, I went to sleep. Never saw the kid again. Next morning, the guards asked what happened. I played dumb.

When I first arrived at Martin County, I was placed in the kitchen dorm. I was instructed to get a locker from a place that resembled a junkyard. The locker was rusted and full of holes. Hundreds of roaches were making a home inside it. There was no way I could store my clothes and personal items in it.

I took the locker into the shower and washed it. A lot of roaches met their maker that day. The holes I patched with toothpaste and toilet paper. I used the pop tops from soda cans – stacked six layers high – to create legs and elevate the locker off the floor. Every time I saw a roach, the locker went back to the shower. It probably got washed more often than I did.

While waiting to go to work camp, I was given jobs to do based on my time at South Bay. Since I had taken and passed classes in upholstery and small engine repair, those were my assignments. In truth, I already knew how to do that stuff, so I paid off the private clerks with food to sign me in and out of the classes. I still have the certificates of completion they gave me.

Having been assigned to the kitchen dorm, I was given bakery duty. Mostly, I saw that the dirty dishes were washed. The dishwasher was a gigantic machine capable of reaching very high temperatures. There was no ventilation in the room and lots of steam which made it difficult to see.

The heat was oppressive. I became dehydrated… lost 15 lbs. in two days. Drinking water did not help. Sweat was a constant. One day I took off my shirt to wring it out, and the CO in charge jumped all over me. No one cared about our comfort or needs.

On my fourth day of KP, two bakers got into a fight in front of a 20-pan oven. They were sent to the box. As much as I didn't want anyone to know I could bake, I realized it might be my only way out of dishwasher duty. If the warden determined my baking skills to be an *institutional need*, it could be the end of my chance for work release, so I was cautious about giving them my qualifications.

At the end of the week, I was reassigned to the bakery where I organized the entire operation. The men already working there had no understanding of bulk production. For the first time, the bakery was run efficiently. I never let on that I had been a baker on the outside. Always gave the credit to somebody else.

You would think that a bakery was a relatively safe place to work. Not in prison. The kitchen mixer was a large machine capable of making 100 lbs. of dough. When ready, I would roll out the dough and cut it into circles much like a doughnut. The blade scraper, which was used to clean the dough hooks on the mixer and the cutting board, was sharp and would make a very effective weapon in the wrong hands. As such, it was kept locked to the table with a three-foot chain.

Early one morning, I was making biscuits when I noticed a food tray had been left on the prep table blocking production. I moved it. The owner of the tray got angry and began cursing at me. He threw a few punches. I fought back, grabbing him by the neck and pushing him over a three-foot separation wall. His legs were dangling in the air.

I told him, "I'll kill you. What do you think of that? I will kill you." His answer came in the form of croaking sounds. I let him go and he ran off.

Later than night, I returned to my dorm. Another inmate told me that the guy who attacked me and his friends were lying in wait. I never went to sleep. The next day was Monday. Monday and Tuesday were my days off. First thing Tuesday morning, an announcement over the PA system requested my presence in the office. When I got there, they handcuffed me.

I pretended not to know why I was in trouble. They took me to the Colonel, who showed me photos of the guy's neck covered in black and blue hand marks. Again, I pretended not to know what they were talking about. The officer relayed events as they were told to him, but he got the days mixed up. He accused me of assaulting the guy on Monday. I said, "Sir, I'm off on Monday and Tuesday."

The officer told an underling to get my schedule, which confirmed what I had said. He assumed the other guy had fingered the wrong person. I was sent back to my dorm. I'm telling you this story so that you understand what an inmate must do to survive. There is never a moment to relax.

I was ecstatically happy once I got to work camp! No job was too hard. I could taste freedom, so I kept my nose clean and stayed away from anyone who looked like trouble. Nothing was going to keep me from going home.

Chipper squad was one of my favorite assignments. Our job was to cut down invasive trees. The officer in charge was named Collins. We had a big ass chipper; it was so dangerous no one wanted to get close to it. I became the guy who threw the trees in to be mulched. If that powerful chipper broke, we got stuck with an older chipper - one that was slow and a pain in the butt to use.

On a day I wasn't working, someone threw something into the good chipper and it jammed. The inside of a chipper is a mix of hinges and springs that work together to pull in the wood and move it through to the blades. The mechanics are complicated, and no one seemed to know how to correct the problem.

With the chipper out of commission, no work could be done, so they took it back to the storage yard in Fort Pierce. For hours, they tried to repair it. They tried everything, used every tool, but the internal workings wouldn't budge.

Collins didn't want to waste any more time. He told the guys to get the old chipper and go back to the job. I had been watching their progress. On a shelf I saw a piece of rebar that I thought might be helpful. Without knowing what would happen, I jabbed the rebar into a little hole in the top of the chipper. Boom! The barrels snapped open, and the chipper started working again. Collins asked, "Why didn't you do that before?" I said, "I thought you guys would figure it out." Truthfully, I had no idea that was the way to fix the jam. I just tried thinking outside the box.

Inside the chipper were two big barrels on huge coils. To clean the machine, you had to lift the barrels and coils out of the way. It wasn't easy. I looked at the new chipper and then at the old chipper. The insides weren't the same. The new chipper had a small hole in a place where the old chipper had nothing. I took a screwdriver and put it into the hole. Like magic, the barrels and coils separated.

Collins was mystified. "I've been doing this job for ten years. I never knew that's what that hole was for."

When I look at a piece of machinery, I assume every part of it is there for a reason. You must figure out what that reason is. It's not academics that make someone a success. It's the ability to be a critical thinker.

Friendships with other inmates were rare. Friendships with correctional officers were rarer. There was one CO, nicknamed Schizo, who was hated by most of the inmates. They thought he was crazy. I don't know why, but he and I got along well. We would talk when out on road crew together. That didn't mean he cut me any slack.

I had been assigned to Schizo only about two weeks when he ordered my crew to whack cattails and weeds along the roadside. Cattails meant there was water nearby, and water meant there would be rats and water moccasins... lots of water moccasins. We were given high boots and told to get into the water. The younger guys took pity on me; they thought I was too old for the job, and I encouraged them to think that way. Schizo couldn't have cared less if Methuselah was on his crew. His attitude was "Get your ass in there."

Had I refused, I would have been given 60 days in the box and would have lost 160 days of gain time. Gain time is the 15% reduction of sentence that is given to each inmate by the state. Sometimes it's referred to as "the third off" of a sentence. Not everyone is eligible for it. I was doing 85% percent of sentence. Eighty-five percent gain time is given for offenses committed on or after October 1, 1995. The provision prohibits the award of any gain time that results in an offender being released prior to serving 85% of his sentence. If disciplinary action is taken against an inmate, they could wind up doing 100% of their sentence. Even knowing that, I couldn't keep my mouth shut.

I tried to explain to Schizo about the snakes... that they were poisonous and aggressive. He told me to mind my own business. Being a smart ass, I said, "You know, up until now if someone started to beat your ass, I would have helped you. Now, you're on your own."

Schizo took that as a threat. He called a report into the main office, but I didn't get into any trouble. Most of the corrections officers liked me... I made them laugh... so they protected me a bit. Even now, three years out of prison, they stay in touch with me.

There was another time... I came back to camp after a long day on the road. My crew and I were in the strip shack (going out and coming in everyone was strip searched – every day) when a Colonel came in and told us to go back outside. We were exhausted and in need of showers and food, but we had no choice. A CO lined us up in the yard and told us to wait.

Forty minutes passed; it was getting dark. The Colonel returned and looked dumbfounded to see us still standing there. He asked,

"Didn't they come to get you?" Jokingly, I said, "Listen. Five more minutes, and I'm outta here."

Much to my surprise, his response was, "You're right. Go!"

Unfortunately, he didn't mean "Go!" as in go home, but by then a hot meal and a hot shower looked good to all of us.

CHAPTER FORTY-NINE

To recap how we have gotten to this part of the story:

Konstantinos "Gus" Boulis, was a Greek national living and doing business in the United States. Among his business ventures were the Miami Subs chain and the SunCruz Casinos line. In 2001, Boulis was shot to death in his car outside his office in Fort Lauderdale. The murder was alleged to be in connection with the sale of SunCruz Casinos.

Anthony "Big Tony" Moscatiello and James "Pudgy" Fiorillo, both Florida residents, were arrested in late September 2005 in connection with the murder. Anthony "Little Tony" Ferrari, who resided in New York City, was also detained in connection with the killing. No concrete evidence could be found, and the case gathered dust for years.

On August 11, 2005, Washington lobbyist Jack Abramoff and businessman Adam Kidan were indicted by a federal grand jury in Fort Lauderdale on fraud charges relating to a disputed $23 million bank transfer used as down payment for the purchase of SunCruz Casinos. Kidan pleaded guilty on December 15, 2005. Abramoff pleaded guilty on January 3, 2006. Kidan and Abramoff were both associates of Anthony Moscatiello.

In September 2005, Federal prosecutors charged Moscatiello,

Ferrari and Fiorillo with the murder of Gus Boulis. Moscatiello and Ferrari were charged with first-degree murder, conspiracy to commit murder, and solicitation to commit murder. Fiorillo was charged with first-degree murder and conspiracy to commit murder.

In May 2006, Adam Kidan made a plea deal with Federal prosecutors. He revealed that Moscatiello and Ferrari confided in him that John Gurino, a known associate of John Gotti, had killed Boulis in a contract hit. Up until that time, Gurino had not been a part of the Boulis investigation. Since I killed Gurino, I was dragged into the Broward County Prosecutor's case against Moscatiello, Ferrari and Fiorello. The case was further complicated by the fact that my trial attorney, David Bogenschutz, was now representing Moscatiello.

Being behind prison walls, I knew nothing of what was happening on the outside. Since I hadn't known Gus Boulis, his death had no bearing on my life. During a prison visit in 2013, my father told me that the Feds wanted me to testify in Boulis trial. My family in New York had read about it in the papers. It was big news in the Big Apple. Not so much in Florida, although the trial was being held in Broward County where Boulis had been murdered.

At the time of the pre-trial hearing, I was at work camp... not on work release. Not knowing what to expect or how long I would be gone, I gave my best stuff to a "friend" to hold. If I had signed it in at the prop room, as was SOP, it would have been stolen.

Each day, I was escorted back and forth from the work camp to the Broward County courthouse. The first time, I traveled in the microwave – a van with an aluminum cage inside to contain prisoners in case of an accident. The cage had a tiny window and a fan that didn't work.

The first time I was taken to Broward, another prisoner shared the space with me, but there was something suspicious about him. For one thing, he was wearing black socks. Every prisoner without exception wears white socks. They are a part of our uniform. When you are in prison, you notice the small details because they can make the difference between life and death.

By some unspoken code, prisoners are usually reticent about talking, especially to someone they don't know. We tend to keep our own counsel. This guy never stopped asking questions. "Hey, you Italian? You testifying in that mob trial?" "Do you know those guys?" "What do you thinks going to happen to Moscatiello?"

I never answered him.

We were driving about an hour when the van stopped at a prison and the guy was taken away. As we were pulling out of the yard, I looked out through a crack in the window and saw him walking across the parking lot with another officer. He was a plant, working for the Feds.

Judge Ilona Holmes presided over the Boulis murder case... both the pretrial hearing and the actual court case. She was assigned to the Criminal Division – 17th Judicial Circuit Court of Florida.

The Pretrial Hearing:

It was about 1 am on a Friday. The guards came to get me at work camp and took me to the main unit. I was strip searched and re-dressed. Shackled. My wrists were secured with handcuffs placed in what is called a "Black Box" or a "Blue Box."

The box is a high impact plastic case with a hinged assembly that can be locked over the handcuff chain and key holes. A chain runs through the box and encircles the prisoner's waist. The chain is tightened and locked so that the prisoner's hands are pulled against his stomach.

The box can cause serious injuries if used incorrectly. There was a time when Florida State prisons affixed the box over handcuffs that had been locked behind the back of inmates merely to move them within the prison. It quickly became obvious that when the box was affixed behind an inmate's back, it caused unbearable pain and muscle spasms that ran up to the neck, even if worn only for a short time.

Inmates began refusing medical and mental health care as well as visits from their legal team to avoid having to wear the box. I saw inmates who had been confined in a box for days. Blood stopped flowing to their hands. Their skin turned white and their hands and arms went numb. It's so painful.

Once I was ready to travel, I sat and waited. I waited for hours. It was about 4 am when Sheriff's Department officers arrived. They put me in a van from the Broward Sheriff's Department. I arrived at Broward in-take and was kept isolated from other prisoners. Eventually, they took me up to the third floor.

The way it works in prison is that the more floors you go up, the worse it is. Higher means you are considered dangerous.

So, I'm in a room on the third floor. Nothing happens over the weekend except that my glasses get broken. I knew not to expect them to get fixed even though I could barely see without them. My glasses were taken away and for the remainder of the weekend, I stumbled around like a blind man.

At 5 am on Monday morning, a guard woke me up and took me across an enclosed bridge that led to the courthouse. Just before we crossed the bridge, we stopped so I could be scanned by a fingerprint imaging system. I put my finger where I was told, and a screen lit up, but I couldn't see what it said because I didn't have my glasses. I could make out the word *CAUTION* and a lot of red writing but nothing else.

I asked the guard what was written on the screen, and he started arguing with me, saying "You know what that says." But, of course, I didn't. Either the guard didn't believe me, or he was a mean SOB.

We start walking again and, again, I was put in a holding cell for five hours. I went to sleep. What else was I going to do. Eventually, two sheriffs came for me. They put me back in the black box and the shackles. We rode the elevator to the tenth floor, where they took me into a room that was connected to the courtroom where the pre-trial hearing was being held.

Looking at the Judge's bench from the gallery, there were two tables to the left at which were seated two defendants and three lawyers. Those defendants were Little Tony and Pudgy. Since Big Tony was under house arrest, he was seated in the gallery. He looked frail and was holding himself up by leaning on a cane. There were television news cameras at the rear of the gallery.

I sat in the jury box waiting for whatever was about to happen. David Bogenschutz approached me and shook my hand. He asked, "How are you, Rosario?" I said, Okay. What's going on?"

David made a motion that suggested he was puzzled by my question. He shrugged his shoulders and walked away. I realize now he probably could not speak to me as it would look suspicious.

The next thing I know, I'm being walked to the witness stand. To the best of my recollection, this is the exchange between Judge Holmes and me once I was seated:

"Hello, Mr. Liotta. We've been waiting for you."

"Ma'am, I don't even know why I am here. I don't know anyone here, and I don't have nothing to do with this case."

"Mr. Liotta, there was a murder in Fort Lauderdale (she went on to give the details of the Gus Boulis case), and you happened to shoot the man accused of killing Mr. Boulis. The dilemma before this court is that your lawyer, David Bogenschutz, is now representing Mr. Anthony Moscatiello. Mr. Moscatiello is accused of ordering Mr. Boulis' murder. The court has a conflict of interest to resolve, and that is why you are here.

Mr. Liotta, you can get into a lot of trouble if you said something to Mr. Bogenschutz in secrecy, and it becomes known to the court. You could do more jail time. There are many things that could go wrong for you here."

"Judge, you can ask me whatever you want. I didn't lie. I shouldn't be in prison. Whatever I said, it was the truth."

Everyone was staring at me, especially the prosecutors. They didn't expect me to be agreeable to testifying because they assumed I was a mob guy and had killed Gurino on Moscatiello's orders. It was rather comical watching them come to grips with the fact that I had told the truth before, during and after my trial.

The lawyers gathered around the judge's bench for about 20 minutes. I couldn't hear what they were saying, but there was a lot of talking going on. When they finally sat down, the judge asked Big Tony, "Do you want to continue to retain Mr. Bogenschutz?" He said, "Yes, ma'am, I do."

With that she addressed me. "Okay, Mr. Liotta, you are going to be with us for a while giving depositions."

The Judge told her clerk to set up a time for me to answer questions. A lot of lawyers were involved. Coordinating their schedules so that all of them could be present on the same day was going to be a long and tedious process.

I said, "Okay," and I got up to leave. A bailiff walked with me since the shackles made it difficult to move. As I was making my way to the door, Big Tony gave me the sign for "Thank you." I nodded in return.

The exchange between us was picked up by the news cameras. Reporters interpreted our actions as a sign that we knew each other and were working together. In truth, Big Tony was thanking me for making it possible for him to keep David as his attorney. My response was merely a courtesy.

CHAPTER FIFTY

The depositions:

*O*nce it had been determined that I would remain in Broward for the duration of the depositions, I was placed in general population. I was worried that the other inmates would see a news report about me and get the wrong impression, especially if the newscaster started spouting nonsense about me being connected to the mob. Nothing happened, but that was sheer luck.

A week or two passed before I was called to do the first round of depositions. The guards came early in the morning and walked me to the bridge between the jail and the courthouse. Once again, I had to put my finger on the scanner. I still didn't have eyeglasses, so I remained ignorant of what was written on the screen.

Once across the bridge, I was taken to a different part of the building than where the courtroom was located. Through blurry vision, I could make out a sign that read *HOMICIDE DIVISION*.

Inside the Homicide Division was a long corridor with secretaries or clerks seated at desks on either side. Behind the desks was a big bulletin type board. Think about any Hollywood movie you've ever seen that takes place inside a police department. There's always a cork board on which photos of the "most wanted" criminals are thumb tacked.

I was staring at the board, but I really couldn't see the images that well. Suddenly, it dawned on me that one of the faces looked familiar. It was me. The photos hanging around me were the defendants in the Boulis case. It was as though I was connected to them.

Eventually, we got to the room where the depositions were going to be held. There was a long, wide table positioned in the middle. There were at least six lawyers and four prosecutors as well as a court stenographer waiting for me.

David acknowledged me by saying, "Rosario, we'll try to get this over with as quickly as possible."

My response was to the point. I said, "Listen, in Martin I'm on DOT in the streets. I use machetes and chain saws. There are women and children nearby. I'm not talking until you take these handcuffs (I was confined with the black box) off me."

David knew that if I didn't talk, they would have to reschedule the depositions and more weeks could pass before they got the answers they were waiting for. One of the men at the table said, "Take the cuffs off of him." Another man says, "No. We can't because he was charged with a murder case." The first man said to the second man, "You get on the phone and get permission to take those cuffs off him right now."

Twenty-five minutes passed. I had a soda and relaxed while we waited. Finally, someone decided that the box could be removed but one hand had to be handcuffed to a chair.

The stenographer was seated next to me. She was young and, I'm guessing, a little intimidated by me. I asked her name, and she told me. I said to her, "Listen, these guys might piss me off. I might say mother fucker this and mother fucker that, but I mean no disrespect to you."

Her eyes were so big. She said, "Oh, that's okay." I felt bad for her.

David got the depositions started. He began by acknowledging that he knew me because he had been my lawyer. "Okay. I know your story, but I still would like to ask you some questions."

Nothing David asked was a surprise. We had covered most of the questions during my own trial. David was well-versed in what I was going to say. Once he was satisfied he had all the answers he needed, the other lawyers began asking their questions. Most of them were respectful and courteous. There was one guy who attended the meeting via conference call. He was a jack ass. Being on the far end of some telephone wires filled him with bravado. I'm sure he wouldn't have been so cocky had he been looking me in the eyes.

The first and only question he asked was, "Mr. Liotta, are you doing this because you're trying to get out of prison?"

My response wasn't very polite. I said, "Let me ask you something. You're a freaking lawyer and you're asking me that question? I'm not ratting anybody out. The court subpoenaed me. I don't want to be here. You're asking me if I want to get out of prison. No. I don't. I want more prison time. You must be the dumbest ass I've ever spoken to in my whole life, and you're a fucking lawyer? Jeez."

Suddenly, he said, "No more questions."

The room was silent for a few minutes. Then, the questioning began again. One of the lawyers asked me to read something, but I was unable to do that because I didn't have my eyeglasses. That prosecutor's name was Brian Cavanaugh. He was the Chief Assistant State Attorney, and he was responsible for bringing me to Broward County to testify at the Boulis trial.

Brian Cavanaugh believed, as did everyone closely associated with me, that the killing of John Gurino had been in self-defense. He hoped that by having me testify at a pretrial hearing, he would be able to convince prosecutors from Palm Beach County that I was a valuable witness to Gurino's character.

Not only did he give me his glasses to use during the depositions, he told me to keep them. He was a nice man.

The depositions took months to complete... months of waiting and one day answering questions – hundreds of questions.

Now, that I had glasses, when I crossed the bridge, I was able to see what was written on the screen. In big red letters: *LIOTTA, ROSARIO CAUTION. HANDLE WITH CAUTION.* It was embarrassing.

I want to explain something to you about prison. Incarceration isn't free, which is a laugh riot (that's sarcasm) when you realize that what has been taken away from you is your freedom. Prisoners pay for their care. The amount breaks down to about $20 a day.

If a parent or friend sends money to an inmate, the system takes a portion of it. For example, if my parents sent me $100.00, I only got $40-$60 of it. The rest went toward my room and board. While I was in the Broward jail, I was exempt from paying because I had been subpoenaed.

When the depositions were over, I went back to Martin County. When the trial started, I returned to the Broward jail.

CHAPTER FIFTY-ONE

The Boulis Trial:

Just before the start of the trial, I was again picked up at the Martin County prison and brought to the Broward Sheriff's jail. I was placed in maximum security. For 23 hours a day, I had a cell all to myself.

The food was great. I wasn't lonely. It was nice not having to deal with any of the insanity you find among the general population. Plus, it was air conditioned. After Martin County, this was close to heaven for me.

At some point each day, I would be notified that I had 30 minutes to shower and get myself ready. My showers were quick, and I used the extra time to make phone calls. One day I would call my wife and the next I would call my parents.

At 7 a.m. on the first day of trial, I was led through a tunnel that runs from the jail to the courthouse. I have a vivid memory of sitting outside the courtroom, handcuffed and shackled, waiting to testify. A female bailiff was standing nearby, and she was using a device I had never seen before. She appeared to be talking to someone, but I couldn't figure out how. I asked her to show me what she was using. It was a smartphone. That was the first time I had ever seen one.

The courtroom was not soundproof. Out in the hallway, I could hear everything that was being said. I heard David making motions on behalf of Big Tony, and the lawyers for Pudgy and Little Tony making motions as well. I could also hear the Prosecutor making objections and the rulings by Judge Holmes.

Suddenly, I heard someone say, "Bring Liotta in." Dressed in my prison uniform and wearing shower shoes, I was brought before the jury. The shackles were not removed. A bailiff pointed me to a seat and said, "Don't look around."

There were two guys sitting behind me and not being able to see them made me uncomfortable. For all I knew, they could be dangerous. The bailiff seemed to understand; he told the two guys to move. They did.

You must remember that at this point, I still had no idea why I was there. Sure. I had killed Gurino and Gurino had supposedly killed Gus Boulis, but what had that to do with me? I felt blindsided.

If I wasn't giving testimony, I was held in a jail cell with the new arrestees, including drug dealers, drunken drivers, muggers and rapists. Seating was limited due to space and the availability of non-urine-soaked benches. I was not about to stand for hours on end so, as a *seasoned* inmate, I pulled rank on the less informed detainees. If necessary, I would threaten someone with a good seat by saying they would get a fist in the face if they didn't move. I never picked on the biggest or the smallest guy, and it was never my intention to follow through on the threat. The inexperienced, as I had been years before, were easy targets. They caved immediately.

While waiting to testify at the trial, I shared space with a vast array of undesirables. There is a story for each of those men but only a few are worth telling. This is one such story.

My favorite seat in the holding cell was in the corner nearest the door. On one visit, two guys were sitting next to me while others were lying on the floor or leaning against the walls. There were approximately 35 men crowded together. One of the guys on the floor claimed to be an American Indian. He was aggressive, daring the rest of us to question his heritage by asking, "You got a problem with that?"

I had a piece of paper in my hand with my name on it. The guy sitting next to me saw my last name and connected it with my cousin, the actor Ray Liotta. He was impressed. The Indian guy heard us talking. He jumped up and tried to grab the paper. He was snarling in my face, lunging for the paper, but I managed to push him back.

Nearly foaming at the mouth, he then claimed to be Italian and in the mob. He said, "Don't say nothing about Ray Liotta. He's my favorite actor. If you got a problem with that, you got a problem with me."

I wasn't looking for trouble, so I said, "Buddy, calm down." The guy wouldn't get out of my face. Our exchange became a tug of war with him pulling at my hands and me pushing him away. Eventually, I pushed his hands up into his face, and he went flying backwards. He hit the floor hard. The guards rushed in and separated us. We were each put in a tiny cell, but the Indian guy could still be heard saying, "I'm gonna kill you, motherfucker."

The guards questioned the prisoners in the holding cell, and they all said that the Indian guy was the first to make a move... that I was only protecting myself. Once they knew I hadn't started the fight, I was brought back to the holding cell.

When it was time to go to the dorms at the end of the day, the guards piled all the arrestees into an elevator. The intake (new) guys had one hand cuffed. Since I was in prison for murder, I had both hands cuffed and chains on my legs. The Indian guy was in the elevator with us. He tried to start a verbal race war with me. I had passed the boiling point; I threatened to beat him with my feet.

There was a good reason for me to be aggressively vocal. I didn't want that guy in the same cell with me later in the day. Luckily, the guards understood and kept us apart. Even so, he continued to make trouble until the guards dragged him, prone on his back, out of the detainment area.

It only takes two seconds for a gang war to start. Words, not weapons, are often the cause. Blink your eyes and you could wind up seeing nothing but eternal blackness.

On one of the days that I was scheduled to testify – this was my third trip to the courthouse - I was kept in a cell for 14 hours. With me were four guys who were obviously from New York. I made it clear from the start that I had no intention of engaging in any conversations. I remained silent through all those hours.

At some point, a Lieutenant realized that we were all there for the Boulis trial and never should have been housed together. He approached the cell and called my name. "Liotta. Get over here." Then, he called the other four guys. "You're here for the mob trial, right? They put you in here together? Did you get your stories straight?" He thought he was being funny, and I saw an opportunity to lighten the moment.

With a smile on my face, I said, "Nah, not yet. I need another 10 minutes with that guy," and I pointed to someone on the other side of the cell. The Lieutenant responded, "Take him upstairs!" and the guards quickly whisked me away.

David got sick a few weeks into Big Tony's trial. Judge Holmes declared a mistrial. Big Tony was 75 at the time and in ill health. He remained free on bail.

Little Tony Ferrari's trial continued uninterrupted as he had his own attorney. According to the Prosecutor, Little Tony, who was Big Tony's underling, had tried to persuade one of his bodyguards to kill Gus Boulis. Witnesses testified that they had seen him near the site of the shooting.

David was replaced by another lawyer, but because Big Tony didn't have any money left, he needed a public defender. That required a postponement to give the new attorney an opportunity to get up to date on the case. It was almost two years before the trial started again and by that time, I was out of prison.

I spent most of my time at the second trial in the lobby waiting to testify. I never heard what the other witnesses said, but it would have been interesting. All the information on John Gurino that was not permitted to be entered into evidence at my trial – his rap sheet

complete with an arrest for murder and numerous battery charges --
was now presented as evidence in the Boulis trial. I should have been
angry, but what good would it have done.

By the time the second trial started, I was out of prison and home
with my family. My testimony took five minutes... maybe, less.

CHAPTER FIFTY-TWO

Going home was my goal from my first day in prison.

Prisoners often try to psych each other out. They say things to each other that aren't true, and which take away all hope of being assigned to the work release program. I lost count of how many times the guys told me I would never get a job on the outside because I had killed someone. Luckily, I never listened to them, but there were some men who took it seriously and got depressed.

Work camp and work release are good transition periods for an inmate, especially someone who was incarcerated as many years as I was. I got my feet wet, so to speak, and I was ready to get back to the real world. Sadly, a lot of guys on work release broke the rules and were sent back to the main prison to start all over. I never understood how a person could work so hard to get so close to freedom and then throw it all away over a bottle of beer or a few puffs on a joint.

I was eager to work and, by working at Gio's market, I could put in a lot of hours. Most days I was on the job from 7 am to 10 pm. That was much longer than prisoners were supposed to be on the outside, but the Colonel gave me the thumbs up. Even though I was only making minimum wage, my take home pay was $1200-$1300 a week.

Half of everything I earned went back to the prison system. One hundred dollars was given to me for my week's expenses. The rest went into a savings account for when I was finally free. The average pay for most men on work release was $200 a week. I was the exception, but I worked my tail off.

As hungry as I was to work, I was also hungry for good food. Unfortunately, the first time I ate a steak, I got sick. I still can't eat beef. Being in prison does terrible things to your digestive system.

The day I was finally set free, my parents, wife and son picked me up outside the gates. We went straight to motor vehicle, so I could get my driver's license renewed. Then, I went to the nearest car dealership and bought wheels. I brushed my knees off and never looked back. There was a new world waiting for me.

Most people think that the biggest adjustment was getting to know my wife and son all over again. Not so. Sheryl and Rosario, Jr visited me in prison every week. I taught Rosario to play chess, and he quickly beat me. We spoke on the phone every night. Our relationship was on solid ground.

The real hurdle being on the outside was not panicking whenever I saw a police car. If I was driving and the speedometer went five miles over the limit, I would start to sweat. I had a few close calls, being pulled over for minor infractions.

Sometimes, I felt like I was in a foreign country because the roads had changed so drastically. I would make a left turn onto a street that no longer allowed left turns. Sirens! It was an innocent mistake. Unfortunately, when a cop pulls you over, he pulls up your arrest record and that sets the stage for how he will treat you.

There was only one incident that proved difficult for me when I got home. Rosario Jr. began to have problems at school. The kids would push him around to see if he was like his dad. He never fought back. I told him he needed to stick up for himself.

My son has never been shy about speaking his mind. He said,

"Dad, I don't want to be like you."

There was a pain in my chest as I heard and felt my heart break, but I didn't want it to show. Kiddingly, I said to him, "If you don't stick up for yourself, you won't have to worry about those kids. I'm going to beat your ass."

Quick on the comeback, he said, "Yeah. That's what got you in trouble in the first place."

We had a good laugh, and I learned to respect my son for his ethics. He is wise beyond his years.

~

By this time, Gio's little open-air farm market had become a grocery store where people could buy soups, salads, cold cuts, and dinner items. I created a lot of the recipes that are still used today.

I'm a good cook. I've always been instinctive of what foods go well together. When I first started back to work, there was only one oven, but Gio, seeing how popular my recipes were with his customers, put in a new kitchen for me. To get the food from the kitchen to the store, we used a golf cart with a trailer on the back. A driver would pull up behind the kitchen, and he and I would load the food for delivery.

Our pizza was and still is considered the best in the area. My brother made the dough, and I made the sauce using Gio's family recipe. The only drawback was that customers wanted to eat in sometimes and the space was too small.

I suggested to Gio that he enlarge the deli area by taking down a storage room wall and adding more tables. Customers could then enjoy pizza, hero sandwiches and dessert in one location. Since the market also sold homemade ice cream, chocolate covered strawberries and other sweet treats it was a perfect mix.

The pizza business grew so quickly that we had to continually buy more ovens. When Super Bowl Sunday came around, it was a madhouse. People were lined up waiting over an hour for a pie. It's still the best pizza in the area, and my brother is still making the dough.

As the market became more popular, the demand for my soups and hot dishes grew. The new kitchen was no longer adequate. Gio added an addition so I would have the space and equipment I needed. I was making gallons of different soups every day, as well as creating simple but delicious "one dish" meals that people could take home.

One of the most popular was my turkey and stuffing dinner. Every morning, I made stuffing using all fresh ingredients, including Italian sausage and cranberries. The stuffing was placed in the bottom of a chafing dish. Then, I layered it with slices of roasted turkey, Yukon gold mashed potatoes, and turkey gravy. Cranberries were sprinkled over the top.

We cut the turkey into good sized squares, which were more than enough to fill the hungriest stomach. Each chafing dish served 12 people, and I was making a minimum of 12 pans a day. The demand was so great, we couldn't keep up. I brought my son Jimmy in to help. We were literally "... cooking on all four burners."

I continued working at the market for a year. The days were long. I was always tired, and I realized that after 12 years in prison, I needed time to myself – time to decide what I wanted to do with my life. Money was a necessity. I took a part time job with a buddy of mine who had a pool cleaning company. I only worked a few days a week, which left me time to spend with Sheryl and Rosario, Jr.

To relieve tension, I went to the gym every morning at 6 am. Readjusting to life on the outside was not as easy as I thought it would be. There weren't many people working out at that early hour, which made it easy to get to know the other gym rats.

I met a man who owned one of the largest commercial truck dealerships in the area – TLC Trucks and Equipment. What a nice guy! TLC carried a full line of new and pre-owned wrecker/tow trucks. The owner was a visionary. He not only sold and leased vehicles, he built trucks to the exact specifications needed for any business.

Side by side lifting weights, we started talking. He offered me a job even though I knew nothing about tow trucks. My lack of technical knowledge could be corrected, he said. What he wanted was my personality... my ability to talk to anybody and make a friend out of them.

Just as in my flatbread cracker days, I went back into salesman mode. I used the same techniques that I had used to get restaurants and stores to carry my cracker line and before I knew it, I was outselling all the other salesmen. At first, I spent a lot of time following the old timers around, learning the business. I also learned how to drive the different types of trucks and passed the tests for my commercial driver's license on the first try.

Waiting for business to come to me has never been my strong suit. I took my job out on the road. For six months, I followed every tow truck I saw until I knew where its home base was located. I went into every company, big and small, that had a tow truck in their yard. From Fort Lauderdale to Miami, I was on the road hours every week making contacts and customers for TLC.

One day, I had a brain storm. I drove a brand-new tow truck to the Hard Rock Casino in Hollywood. The casino hosted the Hollywood Florida Car Auctions. On Wednesdays, Fridays and Saturdays, the place was jammed. There were tow trucks coming and going. Hundreds of them.

When I got to the auction, I looked for a strategic location to park. I found the perfect spot next to a speed bump. Every driver had to slow down when passing me. Usually, the driver's window was open, and I would hand the guy behind the wheel a brochure with my business card attached. A little conversation, and the next thing I knew, I was friends with everybody on the lot. They invited me into the main office, where we would bullshit and have coffee.

Before long, those guys found their way to the TLC dealership. They would see me behind a desk and act like we had known each other for years. Sales boomed. Problems arose when the long-time salesmen refused to share their commissions with me. I may not have made the actual sale, but I was responsible for each of those sales getting made. It was my business card and brochure the drivers brought into the showroom with them.

A difference of opinion arose. I wanted a share of the commission. They didn't want to pay. If there was one thing I learned in prison, it was to know when to walk away. I soon found another job.

I mentioned earlier in the book that it is rare for me to lose a friend. A buddy of mine from my childhood owned a nightclub in Wilton Manor, a city in Broward County with a high population of gay residents. My buddy, Paul, was well-known in the community. He needed a bouncer at his club and offered me the job. After years of working out in prison and continuing my routine at the gym, it was the perfect gig except for the hours – 7 pm to 4 am.

A restaurant near the nightclub had recently closed, and he asked me to look at it to see if it would be a worthwhile venture for them. The place was amazing. Paul met with the landlord and, based on his already successful nightclub and his reputation, the deal was made.

Once *EAT* - the restaurant - opened, I moved from bouncer to chef. In the morning, I would do all the prep work for the day's menu. In the evening, I would change my clothes and become the maître d, helping to expedite orders and keeping the customers entertained. After 18 months, Paul and I decided to go our separate ways.

For me, leaving *EAT* was a blessing in disguise. I had injured my knee climbing to reach supplies on a high shelf. Walking was difficult and standing for long hours was no longer possible. Paul and his partner are now the owners of a new restaurant, equally as successful as his first.

My knee injury needed medical intervention and months of physical therapy. I thought that taking time away from work would be a blessing. I was wrong. Boredom set in very quickly. My nose began twitching, a sign I needed to look for my next venture.

CHAPTER FIFTY-THREE

People who know me would describe me as a tough guy with a big heart. Intentionally hurting someone is never a choice I would make. I prefer words to weapons and, being a good talker, I can help people find the better way to do things. My goal is always to let common sense prevail.

I can be as hard as nails when needed, but the conduct I saw in prison shocked me, leaving a lasting impression. Even now, years after my release, there are behaviors I can't tolerate… the way people treat each other, the manipulation and lies. In prison, I saw what really amounted to people acting like animals. I don't want anything to do with people who are disrespectful to others.

I hope whoever reads this book understands one thing. While I fatally hurt someone… while his wife and children suffered as an extension of the shooting… I did not act without good reason. Justice was not served by imprisoning me.

Despite my tough guy appearance, when I was arrested, I was as unaware as a newborn baby. Anyone on trial in a criminal case must understand that the judge is unimportant. He or she does not determine your guilt or innocence. That's the jury's responsibility.

Depending on the case, four to 12 individuals who don't know you or care about you will decide your future. Whether you walk free or remain behind bars for life is solely in their hands. Very few jurors want to be sitting in a courtroom for days or weeks. They are there because the system will make their lives miserable if they don't appear.

A trial is like a stage play and the jurors are a part of the cast. They are actors playing a role and, for most of them, a high-profile trial is the biggest role of their lives. They have no idea who the defendant is other than what they are told by the prosecutor. The same is true for the reason why the crime was committed. They only know what they are told, and jurors tend to lean toward the prosecution's version of events.

There's a chance one or more jurors might have committed a crime and were never caught. That could work against the defendant. A "better him than me" mentality prevails.

Everything about the jurors should be suspect to the defendant and his attorney. Their clothes, their smiles, what they say, how they behave, if they carry a briefcase... these are costumes and props. They are all part of the script. Most jurors can't understand the charges levied against the defendant or the evidence that is presented. Yet, they are responsible for deciding if he/she will see the sun rise again without bars in front of their eyes.

During the trial, I often watched the faces of the jurors. They resembled the sphinx. Stone still and silent. I had no idea what they were thinking when they looked back at me, but I always had the feeling that my fate had been decided before a word was spoken. Their eyes asked the question, *"If he isn't guilty, why would the state waste money bringing him to trial?"*

And... I wasn't the only person on trial. My family and friends who attended court proceeding were also scrutinized. Defendants don't realize that testimony to their character is being given by those in the gallery merely by the way they are dressed and the attitude they project. If a defendant's supporters are attractive and

have the appearance of money, it could work against them. If their hair styles are different... if they speak with an accent... if they are fat or short or tall or anything that a juror finds offensive or worthy of criticism, that weighs just as heavy as evidence as fingerprints and DNA. Superficial impressions have condemned many a man.

A defendant must be humble. He or she must make the jury like them but knowing how to do that isn't easy. Attorneys should give their clients a class on how to behave at trial. Putting your life in the hands of a jury is not much different than meeting someone at McDonald's and having them determine your future. You could go to jail for life or die because you ordered your all beef patty with mustard and a juror liked his with mayonnaise.

Here's what I learned throughout this ordeal... always be nice to everyone because one day you might be arrested and someone you met in Target could decide your fate. If you were rude to them, you're toast. If you're a phony, they will know it.

In my case, the judge knew I wasn't guilty. He openly stated that shooting John Gurino was a clear case of self-defense. His words didn't matter. Nothing he said was going to sway the jury. I looked like someone they shouldn't trust. I looked like someone who deserved to go to prison if not for this crime, then for one I had gotten away with.

Getting out of prison after 12 years... I had no money, but I still had a family to care for. If not for friends, I wouldn't have had a job. I had a felony on my arrest record. Employers don't like to hire felons. Even people I knew... people who knew I wasn't guilty... were afraid to have contact with me.

My driver's license had expired. The places that were familiar to me looked completely different. I was lost in my own backyard. If my wife hadn't had charge cards in her own name, I would never have gotten credit.

I was in prison so long, the world had passed me by. Advancements are made so quickly these days, we take for granted that everyone knows everything. I knew very little upon my release. I didn't know how to use a computer or an iPad or a smart phone or any of the newest technology. I didn't realize that landlines had gone the way of the dinosaur.

When I went to social security, I couldn't fill out the forms because the process was computerized. Nobody uses a pencil anymore.

Life outside of prison is often harder for people than on the inside. Have you ever thought about what happens to those who can't read and write? How do they apply for government assistance like food stamps and welfare? How do they get a job?

God help you if you need social services. The people who work there... they don't care. They dislike you before they even look at you. From the minute you walk in the door... from the minute they look at your record, they want you gone.

There was a guy on line in front of me at social security. He had a big gold chain around his neck. Only thing, it was made of some cheap metal. The lady at the counter didn't know that. She kept staring at it and giving the guy a hard time. Bravado doesn't help. You must be subservient if you want help.

If a man can't find work... if he's hungry... if he has no place to live and can't support his family, he's going to commit another crime. That's why recidivism rates are so high.

Prisoners need to be educated while they are on the inside. It's too late once they are released. It doesn't matter what crime they have committed. They must be given an opportunity to do more than exist. If not, they are going to keep repeating their bad behavior.

I'd never seen a smart phone until I went to court to testify in Big Tony Moscatiello's second trial. I had no idea what people meant when they talked about Facebook "likes" or how to insert a GIF. I thought Instagram was a new kind of Western Union.

I can't get life insurance because I'm a felon. Insurance companies regard me as reckless and won't sell me a policy. I don't have anything to leave to my family. I'm almost 62 years old and, if something happens to me, they won't have anything, not even enough money to bury me. It's ridiculous. It needs to change.

I'm hoping this book will convince everyone that it isn't the threat of time behind bars that keeps people on the straight and narrow. If you want to help turn someone's life around, give them an education. Teach them a trade. Make them feel proud. The lack of pride and self-esteem does more harm than any weapon known to man.

CHAPTER FIFTY-FOUR

On June 6, 2018 every major news outlet reported that the 4th District Court of Appeal had reversed the murder conviction of Anthony (Big Tony) Moscatiello in the 2015 Gus Boulis case. He will now be given a new trial.

The court ruled that witness' testimony given at trial was inadmissible because it came second hand from Gurino, who was long dead and could not refute the statement. Under oath, the witness stated that Gurino had spoken to him personally and said, "I got the work from Moscatiello."

In their ruling, the judges wrote that while the Gurino statement had been central to the prosecution's case, many witnesses had questionable backgrounds or had been given favorable plea deals before testifying against Mr. Moscatiello.

> *"Given the substantial issues of credibility of all of the major witnesses in the case, we cannot say that the state has shown beyond a reasonable doubt that the error in admitting (John) Gurino's statement was harmless.*
>
> *We are mindful that there is plenty of evidence of Moscatiello's guilt. But our (Florida) Supreme Court has consistently stated that*

overwhelming evidence is not the test, particularly where the erroneously admitted evidence becomes a focal point of the trial."

Big Tony has continued to deny any involvement in the killing.

On September 6, 2018, the Sun Sentinel reported that the 4th District Court of Appeal had overturned the conviction of Anthony (Little Tony) Ferrari in the same case, opening the door to a new trial. The reason given was that the judge in the original case had improperly allowed the jury to hear cellphone evidence that was obtained without a warrant.

The appeals court also determined that prosecutors failed to share relevant evidence with the defense about secret recordings made to implicate a co-defendant in the case.

Ferrari has been serving a life sentence for murder and conspiracy to commit murder. At his original trial in 2003, a jury decided he should not be executed for the crimes. In accordance with that ruling, the death penalty will not be a possibility next time around.

On a side note:

One of the prosecutors who handled the case, Brian Cavanagh, has retired. The other, Gregg Rossman, is in private practice.

Broward Circuit Judge Ilona Holmes, who oversaw the two trials, retired in January 2019. She had served nearly 24 years on the bench.

CHAPTER FIFTY-FIVE

*B*etween the court case and the sentencing hearing, letters poured into Judge Rapp's office testifying to my good character. I doubt he read any of them. I have read them all many, many times. In my darkest moments, past and present, these letters have been my vindication and my strength.

"Thank you" seems so inadequate. I have always cherished my family and friends, but now... Should those good people who wrote so glowingly of me read this book, please know I will be eternally grateful.

Below are a few of the letters, all of which are addressed to: The Honorable Stephen A. Rapp, Circuit Judge Palm Beach County, Division: Circuit Criminal "X," Main Judicial Courthouse, 205 North Dixie Highway, Room 10.2204, West Palm Beach, Florida 33401

Dear Judge Rapp:

This letter is to let you know a little about my son, Ralph Liotta. Ralph is a very caring person. He is very humorous and cheerful, hardworking and loving. I know you have a big decision to make regarding his sentencing. I only hope you consider some of his qualities and traits when deciding his sentence. Ralph is the type of person that would put up some of our workers in his home for the holidays when they were without family in New York. He would take them home to our house for Thanksgiving, Christmas, 4th of July in order to feed them and make them feel at home. Generosity was always Ralph's middle name.

I can remember years ago when we lived in New York during some of Long Island's worst snow storms. My son Ralph would drive the bread truck through hazardous conditions picking up senior citizens who were stranded with groceries and packages waiting hopelessly for a bus that would never come. He would drive them home and help them with their groceries. He was happy just to help them, as he has always enjoyed helping anyone in need.

Ralph has also had his own set of challenges, but always faced them squarely and with a smile. Several years ago, he had a terrible car accident that nearly killed him. I thought for a moment I had lost my son. Thank God he recovered completely. He was ejected from the vehicle and spent over 5 weeks in the hospital. He has also had a number of successful business sales sour because of the misfortune of others. Each time he would simply dust himself off and go back to "the drawing board" despite losing up to several hundred thousand dollars. The most recent setback occurred just prior to his opening the Corner Deli. After working tirelessly to build up a large wholesale bakery operation, the buyer defaulted leaving Rosario empty-handed. How did he react? As he always had. He simply went back to work and opened the deli, just a few doors down. Now because of circumstances of which you are aware, he finds himself facing jail time.

Ralph is critical to his family. He has a sick wife, a two-year-old toddler and two other children. He would always pass by the house each day to check on his wife and baby just to make sure they were okay. Now he cannot do that. In fact, this entire situation has put a tremendous burden on the entire family who must try to support and provide for Ralph's sick wife and children. I assume the state will have to help them as I am 73 years old and my wife is 70. We both work just to make ends meet. We try to help out Rosario and Sheryl as much as possible, but it is hard. We have all to do to help grow up Rosario's oldest boy Jimmy who is a good hardworking boy.

Your Honor, I came out of the U.S.M.C. in 1954, went to work as a baker, and have worked hard ever since. I know my son Ralph to be a hard worker and a good family man. I hope and pray that you are as lenient and compassionate as the law allows when sentencing my son. We all miss him very much. I cannot even talk about him to anyone without crying. Thank you for your consideration, and for reading my letter.

Truly Yours,
Vincent Liotta
Rosario's Father

To The Honorable Judge Rapp:

I am writing this letter to you to tell you a little something about my son Ralph Liotta. From when he was a little boy he was a good baby. Growing up he went to school, played baseball with his friends. He was born in Queens. We moved to North Babylon, Long Island. He was about 3 years old. We were a very happy family.

We had a bread business about the time he was in his teens. Both he and his brother worked in the bakery. My daughter worked in the office. In 1990, my brother-in-law passed away. He (sic) (Rosario) went to Florida to help his aunt with her business. He lived with her for a while. After a while, he went and opened a wholesale bakery. He built it up.

He always helped me and his father. We came down here (sic) (Florida); he made us live with him. I worked with him all the time. He always took care of anything we needed. He is a very good person. He had a car accident and almost died. He couldn't get out of the car. All of a sudden, he said he saw two hands grab him and pull him out of the car.

He had a son after that and named him Rosario Angel Liotta. From that time on, he went to church every morning. In fact, he had the compassion to light a candle and say a prayer for John Gurino's soul despite the fact that John Gurino threatened and terrorized my son for an extended period of time.

He also has a daughter from a previous marriage. They adore him. He is a lot of fun. He wouldn't hurt anybody. I was with him every day through all of this. I could go on and on.

Your Honor, what I am trying to say is please try to be as lenient as possible when you sentence him. I know you will do your best. God Bless You

Joan Liotta
His (sic) mom
To The Honorable Judge Rapp

Concerning the case of Ralph Liotta

My wife, Joan, and I have known Ralph Liotta for almost two decades. We believe him to be a good-hearted person, always ready to go out of his way to help people. He has always been a very hard working and productive person.

We were shocked to learn of his problems. We feel, in our hearts, that Ralph would not purposely hurt anyone. It is our belief that incarcerating Ralph, thereby not allowing him to work to support his family, who need him so badly, would not be of help to society.

Sincerely,
Nicholas J. Lamonica

To The Honorable Judge Rapp:

For approximately 15 years, I have known Ralph Liotta, the eldest brother of my sister-in-law, Emily Scuderi. Over the years, Ralph has worked tirelessly to provide for his family and to serve his community.

He is a committed family man, an industrious business person, and a caring citizen concerned with the well-being of others.

On the morning of Friday, January 28th (2005), as the jury began deliberations in his case, Ralph spoke to me via telephone, not to seek comfort or encouragement for himself, but to lift my spirits as I recover from cancer surgery. Ralph's way is always to help others. Although I know this so well of him, I was never more deeply moved by his generosity of heart than on the very day in which his own life hung in the balance.

Ralph's sincere love of people is evident to all who know him and is a distinguishing characteristic and a guiding principle of his life.

Sincerely,
Donna Scuderi

Honorable Judge Stephen A. Rapp

I first met Ralph Liotta at my daughter's hospital bedside in the Trauma Center at Delray Hospital. My daughter, Sheryl, was not expected to live. The doctors said we could only wait and see. Sheryl and Ralph had been married on June 14, 2001. The date of Sheryl's injuries was July 5, 2001, only three weeks later.

Sheryl was in the Trauma Center for approximately five weeks. During that time, I witnessed the dedication Ralph has to her. He did not want her to be alone, he spent endless hours with her, making sure she was kept clean, talking to her even though there was no response, no movement. Miraculously, Sheryl did live. I honestly credit Ralph with saving her life. She was transferred to Pinecrest Rehabilitation Center. Ralph and I took turns staying with her. He spent night with her, and I stayed during the day.

I can only say that most men would not have stayed with her. He married a beautiful, vivacious woman. In three weeks that woman was taken away. She was not able to walk, talk, eat, nor control bodily functions. He could not wait to get her home, to help her in her recovery.

Sheryl and Ralph have a two-year-old son, Rosario. Sheryl is able to take care of the baby and do household chores on her own. She suffers from a condition called Aphasia, an inability to verbally express oneself. It has been their routine that Ralph either brings their dinner home, or he cooks when he gets home. He is very forgiving and understanding of her shortcomings; he takes care of her.

It will be a hardship for Sheryl and baby Rosario while Ralph is incarcerated. In Sheryl's own words, "He takes care of me. He makes sure I am dressed right. He helps with the baby in the evening. We miss him."

Ralph is a good man; he loves his family and his many friends. I can only pray you will take all of this into consideration when applying your sentence.

Sincerely,
Carolyn Pappalardo

Dear Judge Rapp:

As Ralph Liotta's aunt, I respectfully submit this letter in reference to his case. As you can imagine, our family is in great despair as a result of the recent verdict. At this point, in light of the jury's opinion, we ask that you please consider extenuating circumstances behind this very complicated case, as well as the character of my nephew, Ralph Liotta.

I watched Ralph grow from a young child into a man and consider him like another son. Ralph has always been a dedicated family man and hard-working person. Even as a teenager, when Ralph first started working in the bakery business with the family, he was responsible. Always up early, working diligently, regardless of the fun activities his peers were up to for the day, and never a complaint. Ralph has always been dependable and made our family proud. Without failure, he is a positive person, offering a smile and encouragement to everyone he meets throughout his day, even perfect strangers.

As I watch Ralph's son in the bakery today, I am pleased to say he is trying to be every bit the man his father has taught him to be. The young man is carrying on the long-standing family business of baking, being a tried and true right-hand man to Ralph's father. Jimmie, who is also my brother. All Ralph's children are exemplary individuals and have benefited greatly from his unconditional love and fatherly influence.

I have my own reasons to be especially thankful for my nephew's selfless dedication to family. In 1990, I was left reeling in tremendous anguish from the sudden death of my husband of 39 years. I knew nothing of life without a partner and was nearly rendered helpless by the loss. Despite the fact that he had his own responsibilities on Long Island, N.Y., Ralph immediately came to Florida to help me in my time of need. Ralph lived in my home for two years, supporting me personally, as well as helping me tend to our family business.

Of course, as a judge, you've seem more than I could imagine in the way of defendant's, from hardened criminals to innocent victims and everything in between. I ask that you please consider the type of individual who will sit before you as his case makes its way toward sentencing. Ralph is not a criminally minded person. Ralph's primary goal in life, since he was quite a young man, has been to provide for his family. Our family will be dealt a tremendous blow in his absence. Ralph's parents are aging and need him more than ever and, in addition to his other children, he also has a toddler-aged son, Rosario, who deserve the same attention and love Ralph so graciously gives to all his loved ones.

I ask that you please consider the extenuating circumstances that surround this case. I believe, in all truth, that Ralph's reaction to being threatened was not derived from revenge or criminal intent. Ralph's reaction was the result of genuine fear for his life. This is a provider and a family man, not someone who belongs in the criminal justice system for an extended period of time, where he is helpless to do what he has done for so many years, work hard and provide for the family that is the very core of his life.

I thank you for taking the time to consider my opinion.

Sincerely yours,
Jean Pellito

Honorable Judge Rapp:

My name is Peter Amato. I was a police officer in Suffolk County, New York for 25 plus years and retired as a detective sargant (sic). This letter is on behalf of Ralph Liotta. Ralph's dad Jim Liotta and myself go back some 50 years. We were young boys growing up in Brooklyn, N.Y.

Jim Liotta is a good man, he worked very hard for his family. Jim and his wife Joan have raised a good family. Jim was in the U.S. Marine Corp. during the Korean Conflict and served his country well. He is an asset to his community and his country. The reason I'm writing about Jim Liotta is I'm trying to show the court system the type of family Ralph comes from. I remember when Ralph was born. Ralph grew up in a good community and with a great family. When Ralph grew up and started his own family, he worked very hard and was a good provider for his growing family.

I would like to see our judicial system really look into Ralph's background and take into consideration what he has accomplished in the past. Ralph will not be the only one to suffer. His mom and dad will suffer also. They in turn will be helping Ralph's family. It's said that so many families have been destroyed by this tragic event. Both the Liotta and Gurino families will never be the same and I feel for all of them.

What I'm trying to say, Your Honor, is that I know that the law has spoken, and Ralph Liotta will have to pay for the crime that has been committed. I know you must go according to the way the law is written. All I ask is that you be as lenient as the law allows.

On behalf of Ralph and his family, I remain,

Respectfully yours,
Peter Amato
Retired Police Officer

The Honorable Judge Stephan A. Rapp

I am Ralph Liotta's first cousin and am submitting this letter to you in light of his recent trial. I realize you will soon have the difficult task of contemplating his sentence. In light of same, I would like to interject some observations for you to consider about his personal character.

I grew up with Ralph and he has always been like a brother to me. Ralph is a kind, generous person, who has never failed to be there for me when I needed him. Ralph is the first person volunteer to help you and the last person to remind you that he did.

When my father passed away, I was left with the difficult task of not only dealing with the grief but also with continuing to operate the business we had once run together. At that time, Ralph selflessly stepped up to help me, working long hours and at times for very little pay. Yet, Ralph never demanded kudos or special consideration. That is just Ralph's character and he was merely doing what came naturally.

As a judge, surely you see this world, and our criminal justice system has more than its fair share of people who live their lives without conscious, selfishly regarding themselves over all others and ripping apart so many lives in the process. The actions of such individuals not only cause need to remove them from the general population at times, but they require counseling and guidance so they can re-enter society as more conscious, productive people. I respectfully submit to you that Ralph is not one of these people.

Ralph is not the typical person to be caught up in the criminal justice system. Ralph has a good soul and is a conscientious, hardworking family man. I believe that Ralph does not require any special education on these principles nor is he remotely a danger to the general public at large. Ralph Liotta's long-term incarceration will not prove a benefit to society, but it will prove a tremendous detriment to the family he supports. The unfortunate incident that led to him being a defendant was the result of being drawn into a frightening, emotionally-charged predicament. Ralph's actions were not the result of an evil mind bent on revenge who planned such a horrific crime to occur. Ralph responded out of fear for his own life and that of his family, who had been repeatedly threatened. Ralph's behavior on that afternoon was the result of him being terrified and panic-stricken, not ruthless or premeditated.

Judge Rapp, thank you for considering my observations about Ralph Liotta's personal character. I submit this opinion to you with the utmost respect for your ability to pass an appropriate sentence. I realize your responsibility is not an easy one and would hope insight into the defendant's character could assist you when contemplating his sentence.

Sincerely yours,
Domenic V. Pellito

Dear Honorable Judge Rapp:

I am Ralph Liotta's brother, Anthony. Sixteen years ago, after my divorce in New York, my brother took me into his home here in south Florida and trained me as a baker to build my career. We are a very close family. It would be difficult to imagine our family without Ralph who played such a vital role in all of our lives. He is a wonderful husband, a loving father and a great brother.

I love my brother, Ralph, very much and hope you will consider these comments when evaluating his case in my hope that he will soon be able to return to his loving family. We would be most appreciative if you could find it in your heart to be as lenient as possible when sentencing my brother. Thank you for your consideration.

May God bless you and your family and keep you in his watch care.

Very truly yours,
Anthony Vincent Liotta

Dear Judge Rapp:

I write to you on behalf of my brother-in-law, Rosario Liotta. I have known Rosario in ways that few have for over 14 years. Rosario is a kind, warm hearted, hardworking, generous individual. He is always there for others when they need a hand. He is that way to both friends and family alike. He is truly a unique individual with a special blend of wit, humor, sincerity and generosity that impacts everyone he comes in contact with. Everybody loves Rosario and holds him in the highest regard. His charismatic personality and charm make a lasting impression on anyone he meets.

He is a wonderful family man, who has had to overcome various types of adversity I order to provide for his family. He is an extremely determined hard working businessman who has the responsibility of not only providing employment and support for his older (70+) parents but is raising three children (one of which is hardly a toddler), along with a disabled wife. No small task.

Rosario would never hurt anyone willfully as he cares about people. His heart is good, his intentions always are as well. Just recently, Rosario impressed me once again. As I sat with him in the courthouse cafeteria awaiting the verdict, he spoke with my sister Donna, who was just diagnosed with stage III uterine cancer the same week. He took time to lift her spirits with his wit and humor, putting his own concerns behind him in order to help her. She spoke with me later that day about the manner in which he handled that phone call under what had to be very stressful personal circumstances. This is just a small sample of how Rosario makes a difference in the lives of people.

I respectfully request that you consider these factors as well as the testimony of others when sentencing Rosario. Any leniency would certainly be appreciated by those who cannot imagine what life would be like without him around. Thank you for your consideration.

Respectfully yours,
Anthony Scuderi Jr.
Brother-in-law to Rosario

Dear Judge Rapp:

I was once related to Ralph Liotta through marriage. We were also involved in two businesses together, one in which we were actual partners. I came to know Ralph not only as a family member but also as a business associate.

As a family member, Ralph moved down to Florida in the early 90s and became a loving and helpful addition to my husband's family. I grew to know Ralph's character and found him not only to be devoted to his family and kind hearted but I also found Ralph's presence an extremely positive one. He is a benevolent soul and generous in every way.

As a family, we also benefited by Ralph's willingness to help us with our businesses. I needed to count on Ralph day in and day out and never once did he fail to make a favorable representation of our products, services and company. Ralph's primary goal was always to avoid trouble, to resolve any issues that came up and move on with good will. I would never for one moment to this day fail to trust that Ralph's first intention in all regards is a good and fair intention.

I am expressing these personal observations on Ralph Liotta's character to you because this case has extenuating circumstances and, to say the events of October 2003, were out of character for the defendant, is a grave understatement. I've known Ralph, I've worked with Ralph, and I honestly believe he had to be truly in fear for his life. Ralph has too much to live for to ever plan or want such a horrible event to occur. Some sort of premeditation is unbelievable to me as Ralph is quite simply not that complicated or conniving. Ralph is not a ruthless man, or a man devoid of conscious. Ralph Liotta's reaction and behavior on that fateful afternoon were fueled by the insidious emotions of extreme fear and panic.

I respectfully request that you please consider all the various circumstances which influenced the events of Ralph Liotta's case. This is not a typical person you'd find caught up in the justice system. The events of this case were fraught with powerful emotion. It is my opinion that this world will not be a safer place with Ralph Liotta behind bars. Ralph Liotta was afraid, and his reaction was not that of a criminal mind but that of man in immediate fear for his life.

Respectfully yours,
Valerieanne Martinetti

Dear Judge Rapp:

I am writing this letter to urge you to exercise your broad discretion and grant leniency when you pronounce sentence on Ralph Liotta. In the twenty years that I have been at the bar, I have never written to ask a judge to act in any particular manner on behalf of a defendant awaiting sentencing. I would like to tell you a little about myself and my relationship with the Liotta family as a means of explaining why I am writing this letter.

I have known the Liotta family in excess of forty years. I have known Ralph since we were young children; my family has known his family for many years preceding our introduction. In 1980 my younger brother found himself in a situation not too dissimilar from the instant case. The toll that the judicial process weighed on my family was overwhelming. The events that surrounded my brother's conviction motivated me to enter law school. While in school, I followed his appeal and celebrated the day that his conviction was reversed. In my practice as a lawyer and law professor, I have dedicated myself to the zealous representation of each of my clients hoping to spare them the pain that is all too often associated with finding oneself on the wrong side of a jury verdict. I followed Ralph's trial from a distance and know that the process was fair and the advocacy he received outstanding. He has now reached the point in the process where all of our faith is entrusted to those men and women who are given the title of judge and called upon to sit in judgment of others.

Judge Rapp, I know that your experience is broad, and I am confident that you bring a great deal of wisdom to your judicial role. As a judge you have the unique opportunity to observe society from a vantage point that is not shared by every ordinary citizen. The breath of your experiences most often outweighs that of the lawyers who are entrenched in the very cases they are trying before you. I had the opportunity to speak with Ralph's father after the verdict. His pain was as obvious as that of any man who was soon to be separated from his son. With the greatest personal appreciation for the fairness of our treasured system of justice, I can only ask that you allow your humanity and wisdom to guide you when considering the facts of this case prior to fashioning your sentence.

Thank you.

Respectfully,
Frank C. Corso, Esq.

This last letter was written by close friends and signed by all their children. They asked me not to reveal their names because they don't want credit for doing what they believe was the right thing to do.

Dear David Bogenschutz:

My family and I have known Ralph Liotta for many years. We have known him to be a hard worker and a good friend. Ralph is well liked by all and has many friends who share our family's view.

We have watched Ralph through a difficult crisis before, when his wife, Sheryl, was involved in a terrible car accident. She had sustained severe brain trauma. His dedication to her all through that period was remarkable. Even after her lengthy stay in the hospital, he has shown unbelievable strength and loyalty to her throughout this entire ordeal. Sheryl and Ralph have since had a little boy whom they both adore.

I truly believe Ralph's lack of presence will definitely hinder Sheryl's ability to care for their son. The trauma from her accident has left Sheryl at a disadvantage in which Ralph has helped in a thousand ways. Ralph also has two other children who definitely have been affected by their father's incarceration.

His parents, Joan and Jimmy, who are hardworking, have also been traumatized by this entire ordeal. Jimmy and Joan are loving parents who I have seen throughout Ralph's trial stand by their son.

I personally have never known Ralph to ever even raise his voice or show any aggressive behavior. I know him to be a chipper person, always telling jokes, trying to put laughter into everyone's life.

This letter is my and my family's letter of recommendation to you, which I do not in any way take lightly. I hope this letter to you has been able to let you see the man we know.

ABOUT THE AUTHOR

Rosario Liotta was raised in North Babylon, Long Island, in a typical Italian neighborhood. His dad was a baker and a bookie, a combination which would be an education for Rosario on many levels. Being dyslexic at a time when the condition was still unknown, he wasn't a good student. He dropped out of junior high at the age of 16 and began working full time for his father. Despite never finishing high school,

Rosario had a head for numbers. He was a hard worker and made a success of the many businesses he developed.

In 2003, Rosario opened a delicatessen in Boca Raton, Florida. It was shortly after the deli's grand opening that he shot John Gurino during an attempted shakedown that nearly cost him his life. While the killing was a clear case of self-defense, Rosario was convicted of manslaughter. The Stand Your Ground laws had yet to be introduced in Florida. He served 12 years of a 15 year sentence in prison.

Now a free man, Rosario is determined to tell the true story of what led up to that fateful day, including all the details the prosecution never allowed the jury to hear. That determination is what led him to his co-author, Donna Carbone. A prison guard who had taken Donna's writing course told Rosario, "She's the best writer in south Florida."

Rosario and co-author, Donna Carbone, have a mutually respectful professional relationship and a friendship that will make *Bread and Bullets* just the first in many books to come.

ABOUT THE AUTHOR

Donna M. Carbone is an author and playwright. For five years, her unfiltered opinion column appeared in *The Beacon Magazine*. She is a frequent contributor to the *Jupiter Courier Magazine*. Donna is the author of the Cat Leigh and Marci Welles crime novels set in Palm Beach County. *Through Thick and Thin* and *Silk Suit/Stone Heart* use the true account of her daughter's kidnapping and rape in 2007 to focus a spotlight on crimes against women. The third book, *Total Submission*, is currently being written. She is also the author of *Private Hell,* which focuses on domestic abuse, a semi-autobiographical crime novel. Her first children's book, *Lambie and Me*, is based on conversations with her grandson, Blake.

Donna's play, *Shell of a Man,* was presented at the Dallas Convention Center and the Burt Reynolds Institute for Film and Theatre. Her one-man show, *Fear Sells,* was presented at the TEDxJupiter conference in 2013.

Donna is an outspoken advocate for victims of violent crimes and better healthcare for our veterans. She is a huge supporter of literacy and promotes indie authors in Palm Beach and Martin Counties through her *A Novel Approach to Literacy* author meet and greet events.

"Meeting Rosario and learning more about our criminal justice system has been both a personal and professional blessing. *Bread and Bullets* is just the first of many books we hope to author together."

You can learn more about Donna on her website: writeforyoullc.com

amazon.com/author/donnamcarbone

Made in United States
Orlando, FL
29 October 2023